Walter Reuther

ELDOROUS L. DAYTON

Walter Reuther

THE AUTOCRAT

OF THE BARGAINING TABLE

NEW YORK 1958

THE DEVIN-ADAIR COMPANY

Author of

GIVE 'EM HELL HARRY

9162

For Diane

"The country is passing from the hands of the political goofs into the hands of the labor goons."

H. L. Mencken in an interview

"Yes, I know. In my union there is democracy too—but they know who is boss."

Attributed to David Dubinsky

"We are the vanguard in America of the great crusade to build a better world. We are the architects of the future."

Walter Reuther

"He [Reuther] is an earnest Marxist, chronically inebriated, I think, by the exuberance of his verbosity."

John L. Lewis

Table of Contents

This Is the Man

THE place is Washington, D.C.

The time, Tuesday, October 9, 1956.

The setting, the Old Supreme Court Chamber in the Capitol Building, ablaze with Klieg lights for TV and newsreel cameramen.

One man commands the center of the stage. His flaming hair stands out like a red maple in a forest glade.

He is a man of fighter trimness—a middleweight, or possibly a light heavy, 5 feet 8½ inches tall, 167 pounds, muscular, deep-chested, measuring eleven inches more about the chest than about the waist. The years spent in the gym, the long walks—six or seven miles at night with long, bouncy strides—and the nightly cold showers have paid off, handsomely so. No bulges swell the lean flanks. No gray threads the reddish hair. There are no bags under the small, sharp gray-blue eyes which move from senator to senator on the dais, probing, probing, always probing. Now they light up with quick intelligence. Now they are enfolded in flesh as the man grins. Now he grows angry and they are cold slate lost in a squint.

Until recently he carried in his right hand a small rubber ball which he squeezed and squeezed, again and again, in an effort to restore a part of the strength a would-be assassin's 12-gauge shotgun had blasted out of the arm. Today his hand grips the edge of the table with somewhat its old power. It has a square thumb angle, but the fingers are tapered and uncalloused. They are the fingers of a man who has worked more with his mind than with his hands.

He listens to the senators, he talks with his advisers, bobbing his head back and forth. Again he listens, intently, and takes notes. He is forever scribbling notes, sometimes feverishly. Sometimes he wakes up at night to jot down a thought.

Someone has called him a young man in a hurry, and there is a sense of urgency about him. Watching him, you sense that something impends. He is coiled, like a spring, about to fly off somewhere. You don't know in what direction he is headed, but you anticipate motion, swift, decisive motion.

The senators are about to question him now. He senses it and reaches for the comb in his breast pocket. A neat dresser, looking always as if he had just stepped fresh from a bath, he never wears a hat, and he carries the comb to run through his rumpled hair.

He speaks and his voice is high and metallic. It is this metallic quality other labor leaders dislike in him: the iron will, the tinny personality, the brass nerve.

His instinct senses the hostility of the senators, Carl T. Curtis of Nebraska, Barry M. Goldwater of Arizona. They are questioning him on the use of union dues for political purposes, and his lower lip curls under and protrudes, pugnaciously, like the lip of a bulldog. His eyes narrow to slits in which the gray-blue is almost lost, yet watchful, deep in the wrinkles of flesh.

Senator Curtis is probing now with a lancet of words: "I understand the program was paid for out of union dues by Republicans and Democrats alike, and they had to pay it or lose their jobs."

And the high, ringing metallic voice in reply: "Well, I challenge that, of course. Senator Curtis, you are entitled to your prejudices, but you are wrong on this one."

This is the man. This is Walter Philip Reuther, vice president of the merged AFL-CIO, president of the United Auto Workers, until 1955 president of the CIO, a union of from six to seven millions with a war chest of an estimated $1,000,000,000.

In the give-and-take of the forum he is in his element. On the platform, in the witness chair, before the TV cameras—anywhere disputation is the order of the day—his footwork is nimble.

Senator Curtis calls it purely a matter of political campaigning paid for out of union dues.

No, says Walter Reuther, it is a matter of free speech.

His look is concentrated. He has gathered his strength in his hunched body.

"Senator Curtis," he says, "would you say that *Life* magazine is engaged in political activity when they endorse in a six-million circulation magazine, subsidized by second-class mailing privileges, are they engaged in political activity?"

This give gets under the senator's skin. "Listen," he snaps, "you are not questioning me."

"I would like to have your opinion," Reuther persists,

and now, for all his directness, there is a friendly air in his voice. "I would like to be enlightened about the matter."

"No, you are not—" the senator begins.

Reuther presses him. "Are they? Or are they not?"

The committee chairman, Senator Gore, points out that a member of the senate is not required to answer questions, but Reuther hunches his shoulders in a light shrug, explaining, "Mr. Chairman, I would just like to know Senator Curtis's point of view."

"You know it very well," Senator Curtis snorts. He is seething. "You are one of the most influential members of the Democratic Party."

This, Reuther denies, but the Nebraska Republican ignores him, saying, "You come in here with an array of aides and legal counsel, and your own television setup, and your own motion-picture setup the likes of which have never been seen in the history of Congress."

The neatly tailored, fresh-appearing redhead smiles blandly. He has the boyish look of a lad who wants to trade knives, not look daggers.

"Well, we can't get you people to come on our station," he says, "so we figure we will make a movie and put it on."

Laughter ripples through the Old Supreme Court Chamber.

Senator Curtis has a point of view. He will express it, come hell or high water. "You come here with all this array," he says, flinging a gesture about the chamber.

Reuther breaks in, "Will you come on our stations?"

Reuther's shadow, Emil Mazey, explains, "We would like to ask *you* some questions."

The senator from Nebraska boils over. He lambastes unions. He calls the merger of the AFL-CIO the greatest merger in our economic history. He levels his finger at Reuther—at the TV equipment. "Your appearance here," he cries, "in all this kingly splendor has never been equaled in the history of Congress."

"You dazzle me," Reuther says, and his voice is heavy with sarcasm. "You dazzle me."

And so, questioning, arguing, needling and niggling, quibbling and hairsplitting, Reuther goes on with the show.

Who is this man who flunked high-school English and algebra yet reads only books on economics? Who is this third-generation Socialist bred to worship God and translate brotherhood into Socialistic terms? Did he, in fact, ever quit socialism? Or is the question not whether he ever got out of the Socialist Party but whether socialism ever got out of him?

He is a dedicated man; that, no one can deny. He works long hours, sixteen to eighteen a day. He has no knack for lobby backslapping or story-telling. His strongest drink is weak coffee well diluted with milk. This dates from the night in Munich's Hofbrauhaus when his brother Victor challenged him to down a liter of beer. He has not cared for drinking since that experience. At cocktail parties he takes a Manhattan, eats the cherry and leaves the drink.

He lives simply, for his family and for his work. He likes to do carpentering and to cook. In an unguarded moment he once allowed himself to be shanghaied on a Lake Huron fishing expedition. He went out in the fishing boat once, whereupon his stomach became so squeamish that he stayed in the cottage and read books on economics for the rest of the vacation.

As far back as he can remember he was determined to be a labor leader, and as such he considers almost all employers greedy, reactionary monopolists inimical to the brotherhood of man and blundering daily toward a welfare state.

He has come a long way since the lusty, bawling, brawling days of the sitdown strikes. As one top labor leader has said, speaking of his Socialist-trade-union background, "His early training sharpened him, but it also put him on the wrong tack so far as trade-union philosophy in the United States is concerned. He started out trained in Marxist concepts, and he believed in the elimination of private ownership. He was one of the youngsters we used to call a 'Yipsol' (from Young People's Socialist League). They could talk like hell, but they could not produce anything."

John L. Lewis is blunter in his criticism. He calls Reuther a "pseudo-intellectual nitwit."

A Detroit businessman, George Romney, says, "Walter Reuther is the most dangerous man in Detroit, because no one is more skillful in bringing about revolution without seeming to disturb the existing order of society."

This is the man who conspired with the Communist Party, then tried to shake loose from his association.

This is the fighting redhead who mixed it with Ford Company toughs on the Overpass at the River Rouge plant.

This is the boss of the UAW, who presides at a huge kidney-shaped, light-walnut desk in Solidarity House, the million-dollar-plus UAW headquarters built, ironically, on Henry Ford's old estate overlooking the Detroit River, yet protests against plans to hold the AFL-CIO unity meeting in Miami.

"I can't go to Miami," he says. "It wouldn't look right."

This is the husband of May Wolf Reuther, whom he married on March 13, 1936, when he was a recreation director paid by the WPA. After the wedding he promptly went out to speak at a union organizing session.

Reuther recalls that, after their marriage, they lived in

Detroit's Knickerbocker Apartments. It was a nest of friendly, frenzied CIO officials, an organization which was then a-borning. "We hardly ever slept," says Reuther.

Since the attempts on his life, Reuther and his family have been living in a converted summer cottage on a trout stream "thirty-five miles northwest of Detroit," as UAW publicity reports describe the location. Writers have been asked not to be more specific, and I am willing to go along with the request, although it seems to me that the best way to protect him and his family would have been to say nothing whatever about the new residence.

Reuther's four-acre plot is entered from a public road by a short private drive. The cottage is almost invisible from the public road, but a guest must pass to the rear of a one-and-a-half-story white gatehouse manned by security guards before going through a ten-foot-high steel fence.

Beyond the fence, the route leads across a wide lawn and over a bridge that spans a stream to a tiny island. The path continues across this island to another bridge spanning a swift stream and finally to another island, on which Reuther's rambling redwood-and-glass cottage stands.

Reuther likes to gesture at the water boiling under the bridge and say, "I'm the only union leader who lives behind a moat."

The glass throughout the cottage is bulletproof. So is the glass of the special armored car in which he is driven to Solidarity House since the attempts on his life.

On this moated estate, which costs tens of thousands of dollars a year to maintain, a sum prohibitive for a person of private means, but paid for out of the UAW treasury, Reuther lives like a feudal lord with his wife, his teenage daughters, Linda Ann and Elisabeth Luise, a sheep and two

lambs, two kittens, two German shepherds, a horse, a cocker
spaniel, a parakeet, and a goldfish. He "does it himself"
with a carpenter's kit to strengthen his right arm.

This is the man.

He takes no credit in a personal sense for the fact that he
is a trade unionist. He was raised in a trade-union family.
His father was the international representative of the Brewery Workers Union. Walter Reuther got trade unionism,
the struggle and the hopes and aspirations of working people every day. He never knew the time he didn't dream of
being a labor leader.

He will tell you himself.

"I was raised in a kind of trade-union atmosphere that
said to me when I was a boy that a trade-union movement
based upon principles of pure and simple trade unionism
could not adequately deal with the complex problems of the
working people in the world. . . .

"There is a revolution going on in the world. The Communists didn't start that revolution. It is a revolution of
hungry men to get the wrinkles out of their empty bellies.
It is a revolution of people who have been exploited by imperialism to throw off the shackles of imperialism and
colonization and to march forward in freedom and independence. It is a struggle of the have-nots to get something
for themselves. The Communists didn't start it. They are
riding its back. . . .

"You see, man is an economic being. He has to have
food and clothing and medical care and all the other material
needs, and we struggle to make that possible. But man is
more than an economic being. He is a spiritual being, and
just as food is needed for the economic man so the spiritual
man needs food, and freedom is the food of the soul. The
great challenge in the world is to find a way so that man can

so arrange the relationship of one to the other within one society, and one nation to another in the world society, that we can live in peace and harness the power of technology and exploit our resources and translate that into a good life for everyone. . . ."

Thus speaks this modern Zarathustra, third-generation Socialist, trade unionist, architect of the good life for the brotherhood of man in a united world. Thus speaks Walter P. Reuther.

It is easy to see why he can be a hero to those who have not scratched the surface and seen the political and social schemer underneath; this is the man who has become almost a father image to millions of workers and to whom they look for the secured continuance of their daily bread.

The Architect
of the Future Is Born

W<small>ALTER</small> R<small>EUTHER</small> came into the world on Labor Day eve, 1907.

Whether the birth date can be considered a portent depends on the extent of a person's superstition. Certainly, if the past is prologue to the future, the way was already marked for his feet. Trade unionism and socialism were in his blood. His grandfather, Jacob Reuther, was well known in Germany as a Socialist, pacifist, and labor leader. In 1892 this white-bearded Lutheran patriarch left his native Mannheim for his sons' enfranchisement from military conscription and for his own political health. As their ship sailed into New York Harbor, past the six-year-old Statue of Liberty, Grandfather Reuther stood with his arm about his eleven-year-old son Valentine and said, "A man should always fight for freedom and brotherhood."

Valentine, and later Valentine's children, were raised as Lutherans, members of a faith Jacob Reuther tailored to his own taste. It was his firm conviction that some churches "do too much for God and not enough for man," and he had a saying, "To add brightness to the sun or glory to the name of God are alike impossible."

The age in which Valentine Reuther grew up, married, and reared a family of four sons and a daughter saw the workingman struggle to free himself from the old constrictive relations of master and servant. In later years his second son Walter would say, "We are the vanguard in America of the great crusade to build another world. We are the architects of the future."

The architectural blueprint Walter would adapt to his own purposes was the *Freiheit und Bruderlichkeit*—the humanistic doctrines of German Democratic Socialism, which accepted Karl Marx as early as 1869 and, save for a short period of misgiving when it inclined more to the teachings of Ferdinand Lasalle, remained the repository for the Marxist philosophy in its purest form.

Valentine Reuther indoctrinated his sons with the *Freiheit und Bruderlichkeit* against the pattern of uprising and rebellion in which they lived. Valentine himself had grown to manhood in an age marked by William McKinley's full dinner pail and William Jennings Bryan's Cross of Gold speech. His was the age of the ramparts of Victorian Christian respectability striving to hold firm against the batterings of Brann and Robert Green Ingersoll—of iconoclasm, of image breaking, of tradition smashing. It was an age that saw the Industrial Workers of the World, the Wobblies, attack capital with the weapon of industrial unionism. It was the age of the labor leader, of Samuel Gompers, Daniel De Leon, and Socialist leader Eugene V. Debs. They took on the vested interests, Wall Street, and United States Steel.

Teddy Roosevelt was smashing the trusts. The states were ratifying the Federal income tax, never suspecting that it was a tool which Marx had advocated to weaken capitalism. Everybody was dedicating himself to the proposition that all men are created equal, and feminists were handcuffing themselves to the iron fence outside the White House. Even small boys going to school pounded their feet hard on the pavements and chanted in unison:

> *I should worry, I should fret,*
> *I should marry a Suffragette,*
> *I would die, she would cry,*
> *And she would marry another guy.*

Then came the great bum-busting catharsis of world war, crass and destructive, and, after the cleansing, the Big Rebellion of Youth—Prohibition, bathtub gin, raccoon coats, and hip flasks, and breastless, grinning, bobbed-hair women in potato-sack dresses and roll-top stockings.

Of this rollicking current of events the Reuthers were strangely detached observers. There was no more ardent admirer of Eugene Debs than Valentine Reuther. In 1917, the Socialist Party led by Debs told workers the only struggle which would justify the workers in taking up arms was not America's struggle but the class struggle. The workers were assured that now might they throw a monkey wrench into the machinery of production. Now might they slow up and loaf on the job. When Debs landed in the Federal Penitentiary at Moundsville, W. Va., for sedition, he was only a piece down the Ohio River from the Reuther home in Wheeling, and Papa Reuther took his son Walter on a pilgrimage to see the great man in his cell. The impression of that visit would remain with Walter Reuther through the years.

In Wheeling, where Valentine raised his family and lives to this day, he became at twenty-three the president of the Ohio Valley Trades and Labor Assembly. When his second son Walter was born on that Labor Day eve in 1907, Valentine was working in a Wheeling brewery for $1.50 a day and running the local union.

As each of the Reuther boys came into the family circle, he acquired the main characteristics of the Reuther family, a great capacity for righteous indignation, a feeling for the downtrodden and a faith in the possibilities of social amelioration. For the Reuthers, the six days were work days, but the Sabbath was not merely a day of rest. In many ways it was the most important day in the week. First of all, there was the inevitable Lutheran service, then Sunday dinner, and, when the stacked dishes had been turned over to the distaff side, adjournment to an upstairs back bedroom for dissection of the preacher's sermon.

Not since the days of the Scholastics had there been such polemics. The Reuthers took turns attacking and defending, and no matter on which side a member found himself, he debated with skill and ardor and gained artistry in the niggling type of disputation which characterizes the Socialist dialectic.

Those Sunday afternoons were spent not only in dissecting the preacher's sermon but in discussing the issues which agitated the 1920s, and the practice in controversy schooled Valentine's sons to consider and debate problems quite beyond the intellectual range of the American boy. The back bedroom in the Reuther house heard arguments pro and con on such questions as labor's right to organize, child labor, military conscription, woman's suffrage, prohibition—in fact, whatever subject Papa Reuther had assigned them as the topic for the week.

The Reuther boys prepared their debates at the Wheeling Public Library. Valentine Reuther had fought bitterly against a Carnegie grant for it. He waged the fight in memory of the union soldiers—not the boys in blue, but the strikers who had fought the Carnegie Steel Company at the Homestead mill.

In the debates the four boys, Ted and Walter, Roy and Victor, all redheaded and blue-eyed, were tense and eager participants. As a matter of hard fact, Walter, second oldest, was considered the least eloquent in the furious contests which Papa Reuther refereed sitting on the bed in the back bedroom. The three others shouted and gesticulated in the accepted forensic fashion, but Walter remained calm and analytical and usually wore a confident smile as he quietly told off his points. Usually, but not always. Sometimes his blue eyes narrowed to slits, a sign that he was angry and hurt inside at the extent of man's inhumanity to man and longed to right the wrongs in the general scheme of things.

All this does not mean the physical side of Walter's boyhood was entirely neglected. He might debate child labor or woman's suffrage. His father might take him on a pilgrimage to see Eugene Debs in the Federal Penitentiary at Moundsville. Still, young Reuther was in many respects a perfectly normal boy. He liked basketball and organized a team which won the championship of its class in a three-state tournament. Like most boys he would take a dare. Once he leaped on stilts fom a freight car into a bank of clay. On another occasion he sealed water in a can of carbide and buried it in the ground. The resulting explosion blew the top off a small knoll.

But, as Reuther himself has said repeatedly, he was

raised in a "kind of trade-union atmosphere." Except for a short time when he thought of being a farmer, there never was a time he dreamed of being anything but a labor-union leader. The simplest pleasures of the Reuthers were tied in with the labor movement. When they went on a picnic, it was a union picnic on Wheeling Island. When they went to a social, it was to a social at the union hall.

In a household marked by typical German immigrant cleanliness and orderliness—in an atmosphere that was intensely serious, politically self-conscious and socially extroverted—under a roof where the sect was Lutheran and the creed was the Gospel according to Marx—Walter Reuther grew to manhood.

It is hard to determine today how much Marxism Walter Reuther accepts as such and how much he accepts as a necessary adjunct of trade unionism. One fact not clearly understood by contemporaries is that socialism and trade unionism have come down the years hand in hand. Both are products of revolt against capitalism. The year Marx first saw the light of day was 1818, when Europe was paying the price, economically, politically, and socially, for the long, bloody, and costly Napoleonic Wars. It was a time of volcanic unrest, when the dark cellars and kennels of Berlin, Vienna, and Budapest were spawning the breed that, thirty years later, would follow Lajos Kossuth and his kind to the barricades.

The vines of trade unionism and socialism are curiously entwined. The revolt against working conditions played a great role in early socialism in Germany and syndicalism in France. Daniel De Leon's whole philosophy was revolutionary industrial unionism. Eugene Debs and William Z. Foster were Socialist and Communist party leaders as well as labor bosses. To appreciate the part such basic Socialist principles as the class struggle and abolition of capitalism have played in the modern labor movement, one has only to study the constitutions of such unions as the Amalgamated Clothing Workers, the Amalgamated Textile Workers, and the International Ladies Garment Workers Union.

Into the preamble to the original constitution of the Ladies Garment Workers, for example, was written:

"Resolved, that the only way to secure our rights as producers and to bring about a system of society wherein the workers shall receive the full value of their product, is to organize industrially into a class-conscious labor union politically represented on the various legislative bodies by representatives of a political party whose aim is the abolition of the capitalist system so that we may be able to defend our common interests. . . ."

In other words, the original purpose of the International Ladies Garment Workers Union was the overthrow of our economic system. Reuther has two close friends in the labor movement. Perhaps James Carey of the Electrical Workers is his closest friend, but David Dubinsky, the president of the International Ladies Garment Workers, is almost as close, and Dubinsky's work in the Liberal Party is interesting in view of that ILGWU Constitution.

The discontent and unrest which has boiled up since the French Revolution, producing some material gain but also destroying much that men of culture and substance have held dear, brought to the top the political and philosophical accident we know as Karl Marx. The Little Monster of Trier, born, incidentally, in the same year Mary Shelley published *Frankenstein,* was a social and economic failure who sponged on relatives and friends, stole economic ideas, infiltrated existing radical groups of workers, and drove out the founders and leaders with vile lies and threats.

This man teamed up with Friedrich Engels, an English textile manufacturer's son, to turn out the basic Socialist books. Engels was a Dr. Jekyll and Mr. Hyde character who kept saddle horses and rode to hounds but who, not unlike many of today's so-called liberal offspring of wealthy parents, liked to dabble in radical movements. Engels fell in love with an Irish redhead named Mary Burns, and when darkness fell he would take off his red hunting coat, assume old clothes and a love of the English workingman, and go slumming with his paramour.

Until he came into his full inheritance, Engels even stole from his father's till to support Marx during the years the latter worked on *Das Kapital*. Unwanted in any Continental city, an outcast from his own radical movement, Marx holed up in two dirty, poorly furnished rooms in the Soho section of London with his books and his notes from the British Museum, his wife, eight children, and an old family retainer of his father-in-law's. He rarely washed, or combed his hair, and almost never changed his linen. His children were so neglected that only three of the eight lived to maturity, and two of the three killed themselves, one in a suicide pact with her husband.

But always he pushed ahead on *Das Kapital*. Engels had advised him to write "a big book," because it would be more impressive. "Add to the number of pages by sheer force," he said, "and fill them with quotations that will cost you nothing."

And Marx had said, "I am stretching this volume out since those swine of Germans reckon the value of a book by its cubic content."

It is not hard to understand why Marx has had so great an effect on the trade-union movement. His work is the bible of the workingman. In it, the workingman could find expressed all his resentment against the cruel fate that made him live by the sweat of his brow. At the outset, Marx discarded all morals, ethics, and laws. These constituted a whip with which the propertied class ruled the workers. Capitalism was theft. All profit was unpaid labor hours stolen from the workers.

Couldn't the world see the obvious? All real value was created by labor and must be measured by the wages paid out to the workingman. The difference between the wages paid out and the amount collected from the customer was surplus value. As such, in the Marxian scheme of things, it had no ethical justification.

Upon these basic and, to us, fallacious beliefs Marx erected his fragile structure and cemented it with his dialectic. From birth he was argumentative. Carl Heinzen describes him at twenty-five as small and weakly in physique, with coal-black hair and a yellowish complexion. His nose and face were so broad that his father, a freethinker who had refused to be a rabbi like his forebears, nicknamed him The Moor. Karl's ears stuck out like thick fins alongside his small piglike eyes. It was his habit to sit in a Cologne tavern, alone at a table because everyone despised him; drunk on red wine, he would spit out at each passerby, "I'll annihilate you! I'll annihilate you!"

Such was the patron saint of Communist Russia and the creator of the system which has influenced the pathway of trade unionism and Walter Reuther.

The Other Red Thread

Socialism is only one of two red threads that run through the history of trade unionism, the second being the red thread of violence. The organizer of the great steel strike of 1919, William Z. Foster, who later was to become chairman of the American Communist Party, once said strikes would never become successful unless put on a war footing.

They must, he said, "be organized with all the scientific preparation of a military campaign, with a trained commissary department, shock troops, labor liberty loans, conscription of strikers' families, and all the material, financial equipment, and propaganda necessary to wage a modern industrial war."

Valentine Reuther knew and understood these things. He knew the class struggle behind the Homestead riot, and

because he knew it he fought hard against a Carnegie en-
dowment for the Wheeling Public Library. The Herrin
massacre came when Walter was fourteen, and from his father's lips, as he sat beside his brothers, he heard the trade
unionists' vindication for the terrible vengeance they had
taken.

Papa Reuther spoke to his children with knowledge of
the past. Violence had been part and parcel of the trade-
union movement from its inception as a natural corollary of
the industrial revolution. This was necessarily so because,
under English Common Law, any combination of workmen
in restraint of trade was illegal. It could be punished by
death as it was under the Frame-breaking Act, against
which only Lord Byron's voice was raised in the entire
House of Lords.

There is no doubt that many early factory owners exploited workers. In the England and America of 200 years
ago it was standard practice for the master to abuse his
servant. Any worker's life was a hard one. Long before
dawn, at 3 or 4 A.M., the streets of London echoed to the
clatter of the slop wenches and scullery maids going to work
with their coppers and kettles. They toiled all through
the day and until long after dark. Carpenters worked regu-
larly from seven to seven, twelve hours a day, six days a
week, and were paid off in the taverns so that their masters
could get a kickback from mine host of The Fallow Field
or The Biting Flea. Sweeps, crooked and consumptive,
crisp black and covered with sores, looked forward to about
seven years of life, and that might be suddenly shortened
if they became caught in the narrow flues of a register stove
and their masters were not there to light fires, burn their
bottoms and help them wiggle free. Our 17th President,

Andrew Johnson, a tailor's apprentice, was chained to his table and shears at the age of ten.

From the sloppy, sentimental writings of the Rev. Philip Gaskell, William Cobbett, and others who set the tenor of social comment for the next century and a half, historians have assumed that exploitation of workers came with the industrial revolution along with the spinning jenny and the steam engine. The truth of the matter is that life was hard because the worker's productivity was low, and, except for the propertied class, men, women, and children toiled long hours at hard labor, no matter what their occupation, earning no more than a few coppers and surviving starvation only to die prematurely of any one of many diseases.

It is hard for us to look back and put the world in perspective as it was in 1776. In that year, which saw also the birth of our independence, James Watt rediscovered an old Greek invention, the steam engine, which would take a great deal of drudgery out of man's work.

In the same year Adam Smith wrote *The Wealth of Nations,* in a sense as revolutionary as any part of the industrial revolution. Up until that time we had had a mercantile society, with each state trying to accumulate all the gold reserves it could. Adam Smith pointed out that if man strove for an economic society, in which every individual could advance himself, then the whole would advance proportionately to the sum of its parts.

America had such a society, and most of the immigration of the nineteenth century brought people who were anxious to advance themselves in just such a society. There were, however, a few exceptions, such as the Reuthers. They brought with them only the old class hatred they had known in Germany. Blinded by the injustices of the past, they could not look ahead into the bright future. And this is one thing which must be kept constantly in mind when observing Walter Reuther.

From time immemorial the workers had sometimes rebelled against their lot, as even Wat Tyler's peasants and others had rebelled five and six hundred years ago. The trade union was one form of expression that rebellion took. In 1741 and 1742 journeyman bakers struck in New York City; in 1796 and 1798 journeyman shoemakers followed suit. By arresting the ringleaders, New York constables broke up a seamen's strike in 1803. One of the most notable strikes was that of female shoebinders in Lynn, Mass., in 1834.

Workers got little out of these early strikes and lockouts save broken heads, jail sentences, and hunger pains. As fast as workers, bitter and resentful, quit their benches, others were recruited from the endless ranks of the miserable to take their places.

Unionists tried to fight back by making their organizations bigger and stronger. The International Association of Working Men was the first attempt to organize a union on a national scale. The Noble Order of Knights of Labor, organized on the same lines as the Masonic Order, came to grief in the Hocking Valley walkout, which also smashed the power of the Amalgamated Association of Miners, and the Knights of Labor are remembered today only for having established Labor Day as a holiday.

The third attempt at organizing on a national scale was the American Federation of Labor, which was successful almost from the day in 1887 Samuel Gompers founded it.

Another method of fighting back was the secret society, such as the Molly Maguires. This was a revival in Pennsylvania of an organization whose members, carrying green ribbons to identify themselves and hence called ribbonmen, frequently disguised themselves as women to prevent eviction of tenants.

The American version of the society sought to intimidate Welsh, English, and German miners and rid the coal region of mine superintendents, bosses, and police. The Molly Maguires gained strength during the Civil War. They brought in assassins who could murder, burn, pillage, and assault without fear of recognition, and by 1875 they had gained more complete dominance over the mining class than the Ku Klux Klan ever had in the South.

In that year they forced a general strike on the area.

To meet the threat, Franklin B. Gowen, president of the Philadelphia and Reading Coal and Iron Company, retained a Pinkerton detective named James McParland to break up the Molly Maguires. McParland joined the society, worked with its members for two years, and became secretary of the Shenandoah Division.

In 1892, when the Reuthers came to the coal country, the names James McParland and Judas Iscariot were still synonymous. The miners blamed McParland not for being a Pinkerton but for accepting the shelter, the food, and the affection of the Molly Maguires only to turn state's evidence against them. They even went so far as to charge that McParland, as an officer of the Molly Maguires, had urged them on to greater violence and then had informed against them.

On McParland's evidence, fourteen Molly Maguires were hanged. Others went to jail. The Molly Maguires were smashed forever, but violence in the coal fields did not end with them. For a half century afterward the coal fields would be a labor hotbed. Never did the flames fly higher than they

did during the Homestead battle of 1892, when Valentine
Reuther was only eleven, and the Herrin massacre of 1922,
when Walter, his son, was only fourteen.

Other memorable strikes preceded Homestead and Herrin. During the railway strikes of 1877 the Maryland and
Pennsylvania militia sympathized with the strikers, and in
Cincinnati, Toledo, and St. Louis mobs of toughs closed
the shops, factories, and rolling mills. In other cities, police dispersed ugly crowds before the riots got out of hand.

In 1885 and 1886 there were bitter fights over the
eight-hour day. In Chicago, strikers beat strikebreakers, police beat strikers, and anarchists excited both. On May 3,
1886, there was a riot at the McCormick works in which
several were killed. The following day, when police tried
to break up an anarchist meeting in the Haymarket, a
square on Randolph Street, a bomb killed seven police and
wounded sixty-six. Eight anarchists were convicted of the
crime, and August Spies, Adolph Fischer, George Engel,
and Albert R. Parsons went to the gallows.

In the Homestead battle the student of labor history
finds some justification for Jay Gould's rather cynical statement that one half the common people can be hired to
murder the other half.

The dispute, which colored Valentine Reuther's thinking and, through him, Walter's, commenced over a wage
adjustment and quickly grew bitter. On the morning of
July 5, 1892, steel workers, well liquored up over the Glori-
ous Fourth, seized the Homestead works of the Carnegie
Steel Company near Pittsburgh and made up their minds to
hold fast, come hell or high water.

Officers of the company, every bit as determined, hired
300 Pinkerton detectives to storm the works and dislodge
the more than 1,000 workers entrenched there. Approach-

ing on the river in two barges, the Pinkertons tried to make a landing on the bank to assault the works. The entrenched workmen kept up a galling fire with rifles and pistols. A ten-pound brass cannon behind a rampart of railway ties spewed scrap iron on the men in the bowlers. Hoses were employed to spray oil on the river. It was set afire, and in the eerie light the battle went on until the Pinkertons, caught between two fires and with seven dead and more than thirty wounded, gave up the unequal struggle and surrendered under a flag of truce.

Next day the exultant workers ranged through Homestead like drunken cowboys on payday. There was fighting all through the little town. Men were beaten, women were raped; stores, stoned and looted. Eleven died in the street fighting before militia occupied the town and restored order on July 10.

It was during the railway strike, two years later, that Eugene Debs became one of the household gods of the Reuther family. Debs led the American Railway Union to join workers of the Pullman Company in a sympathy walkout. There were cases of riot, intimidation, assault, murder, arson, and burglary. Debs was arrested on a charge of conspiracy to kill, but Clarence Darrow, who later was to become a noted criminal lawyer, got him acquitted. Later, Debs was convicted of contempt of court for violating an injunction and sent to jail. President Grover Cleveland called out Federal troops, and the strikers, with Debs out of the way, soon settled down and the strike collapsed.

The Amalgamated Association of Iron, Steel, and Tin Workers, which had been responsible for the Homestead strike, called a walkout against United States Steel on July 1, 1901. But, with the turn of the century, there had come a change in union tactics. There was also a shift in the wind, for America was moving from the philosophy of individualism and *laissez faire* toward government action and intervention in the everyday life of the citizen.

Some leaders of American unions, notably Gompers, had long felt they could gain more ground working with progressive leaders than they could working against them. In Theodore Roosevelt they had a President who prided himself on his progressive ideas, and when the United Mine Workers struck against anthracite operators in 1902, the nation saw its executive head intervene for the first time in a labor dispute.

His methods were high-handed to say the least. T. R. told the operators, agree to arbitration or I'll seize your mines. In distant Harvard, even young Franklin D. Roosevelt wondered at this. "In spite of his success in settling the trouble," he wrote, "I think that the President made a serious mistake in interfering—politically, at least. His tendency is bound to be a bad thing, especially when a man of weaker personality succeeds him in office."

William Howard Taft succeeded Roosevelt, and then came Woodrow Wilson, a progressive of T.R.'s stripe, only more so, and the unions, with a strong friend in the White House, expanded their national membership to more than 3,000,000 before World War I.

Still, years of bloody fighting lay ahead of labor organizers. As long as Wilson was President, industrialists knew they would get little help from that quarter. The result was that they hired strong-arm men to do their fighting for them. Out in Colorado, for example, officers of the Colorado Fuel and Iron Company brought in the Baldwin-Felts Detective Agency. The dispute produced sadists on both sides. Some detectives rode about in an armored car shooting down strikers. They got injunctions and indictments against union organizers. They kicked miners and their families out of company homes into the freezing Colorado winter.

When the union set up tents for the evicted miners, Major Patrick Hamrock and a company of state militia attacked the tent city. *The New York Times* reported, "The Ludlow Camp is a mass of charred debris and buried beneath it is a story of horror unparalleled in the history of industrial warfare. In holes that had been dug for their protection against the rifle fire, the women and children died like rats when the flames swept over them. One pit uncovered this afternoon disclosed the bodies of ten children and two women."

In 1920, while the Reuthers watched, the Baldwin-Felts Agency came into West Virginia to keep the unions out of the coal fields. In Matewan, down in Mingo County, the agency met its match, for there Sid Hatfield, of the feuding Hatfields and known as the Terror of the Tug, was chief of police. Hatfield sided with the miners and on the morning of May 19, Albert Felts and his men tried to put Sid Hatfield under arrest. The next few minutes transformed Matewan's main street into a hail of gunfire. It was a battle that would have done credit to a horse opera on TV.

In the first exchange of gunfire Albert Felts and his brother Lee went down. As the former lay writhing in the street somebody administered the *coup de grâce*. Five other detectives fell. Mayor C. C. Testerman of Matewan died with a slug in his belly. Two miners fell with him, and a ricocheting bullet hit and killed a boy bystander.

By August 24 a so-called citizens' army of 6,000 armed and disciplined miners, accompanied by nurses who wore UMWA instead of the accepted red cross on their armbands, marched and countermarched against 2,000 well-armed strikebreakers, detectives, and hired guards. The two opposing forces came to grips at Madison in a pitched battle which the press covered with their ace war correspondents. Who won the battle is a matter of opinion.

No one knows how many died and were buried in unmarked graves. But the Reuthers read every account of it they could get, and that skirmish, fought in 1920 when Walter was twelve and in a formative stage, did much to shape his future.

Almost as much as Herrin, which came two years later.

Walter Makes a Choice

<hr>

Iɴ 1922 Walter, then fourteen years old, **was** hoping to graduate from grammar school and go on to Wheeling High School. By this time the Reuthers were feeling the postwar slump. The cost of living had gone up sharply, and it was hard to stretch the wages of a brewery truck driver to cover the needs of a family with five active, growing children. Ted, the eldest, had taken a job in the paymaster's office at the Wheeling Steel Corporation, and Walter was carrying papers after school to help the family budget, but income never quite seemed to meet outgo.

On April Fool's Day, 1922, when most other kids his age were playing practical jokes, Walter walked his route hurriedly because he knew his father would be interested in the boldface headlines. John L. Lewis, the gloomy, beetle-browed, bushy-haired angel of destruction, had ordered a nationwide coal strike.

Valentine Reuther looked troubled as he read the paper Walter brought him, saying, "This time there's going to be trouble."

Walter's father knew John L. Lewis as a law unto himself. No man could say that the boss man of the mine workers was Communist, Socialist, or murderer. He was above communism, socialism, and murder, at least above them in the sense that he used Communists and Socialists, and condoned murder, to gain his own ends.

As head of the United Mine Workers, Lewis had been a brutal dictator who ran the union to suit himself. He ran the American Federation of Labor to suit himself, and he ran the Congress of Industrial Organizations until that organization ran him out. As a negotiator at the bargaining table he was an unmitigated bully. He has had a phenomenal knack for saying the bullying, unpitying thing at the right time, as he did when he branded John Nance Garner as a "poker playing, whisky drinking, labor baiting, evil old man," killing Garner as a political force and opening the way in 1940 for Henry A. Wallace to become Franklin D. Roosevelt's running mate.

All that spring, Walter followed strike developments in the papers he carried on his route. The meaning of school dwindled to almost nothing, because he was learning more from the strident headlines and his father's interpretation of the newspaper articles.

All the time the situation was growing more serious, and on June 19, just before school closed, newspapers told of real trouble brewing in Herrin, Ill. It seemed that William J. Lester of Southern Illinois Coal had hired C. K. McDowell and a gang of steam shovel operators to work off

the top coverings of his idle coal beds, and Lewis had sent
the following telegram to Illinois State Senator William J.
Sneed:

> Your wire of 18. Steam Shovel Men's Union was sus-
> pended from affiliation with the American Federation of
> Labor some years ago. It was also ordered suspended from
> the mining department of the American Federation of
> Labor at the Atlantic City Convention. We now find that
> this outlaw organization is permitting its members to act
> as strike-breakers at numerous strip pits in Ohio. This or-
> ganization is furnishing Steam Shovel engineers to work
> under armed guards with strike-breakers. It is not true
> that any form of agreement exists by and between this
> organization and the mining department of any other
> branch of the AF of L permitting them to work under
> such circumstances. We have, through representatives, of-
> ficially taken up this question with the officers of the
> Steam Shovel Men's Union and have failed to secure any
> satisfaction. Representatives of our organization are justi-
> fied in treating this crowd as an outlaw organization and
> in viewing its members in the same light as they do any
> other common strike-breakers.

Valentine Reuther shook his head as he read the text
of John L. Lewis's telegram. It was strong language to send
into a town like Herrin, where men were rough and life
was cheap. For years there had been an undercover war in
Williamson County between the Ku Klux Klan and the
men who fought the Klan. Guns had blazed in the streets of
Herrin, and the county became known as "Bloody Williamson County."

In the spring of 1922, when the miners struck for $7.50

a day, the profit of coal operators had fallen off to less than three per cent on their investment, and they felt they could not afford to pay higher wages. At the Lester strip was a huge steam shovel which had been used to help dig the Panama Canal. In charge of the strip was C. K. McDowell, who had broken strikes in Kansas and had his leg broken in turn. He walked on a wooden leg.

When McDowell was taking the top covering off the beds with a steam shovel, the miners began to picket on June 15. Three days later came the exchange of telegrams between Lewis and Senator Sneed. Even as Valentine Reuther read the text of the telegrams on June 19, a Monday, there was a mass meeting of the strikers at the Sunnyside Mine. The Lewis telegram was read which called the steam-shovel men "common strikebreakers."

Two days later, another mass meeting was held in a cemetery at Herrin, and again the Lewis telegram was read. When the miners left the meeting they raided three hardware stores in Herrin and stole revolvers, rifles, and 5,000 rounds of ammunition. A raid was made on the county judge's home but was beaten off. In nearby towns the miners were more successful. Storekeepers were bound and gagged, and guns and ammunition, where found, were carried away by the looters.

The attack on the Lester mine was touched off that afternoon. At signs of the gathering storm, McDowell phoned the county sheriff but was told the sheriff was absent "on official business." The steam-shovel men and armed guards had a machine gun. The cover was ripped off as the strikers advanced and the gun's staccato hammering drove off the early attacks.

But word had gone out among the miners, and from all over southern Illinois they gathered during the night. The mob thought and acted as only a mob can. It was a pack hungry for the kill. The miners came in battle lines, concentrating the fire of more than a thousand rifles and pistols on the embattled steam-shovel men. A hired airplane bombed the mine with dynamite. The explosions blew up a pumping station that supplied water to the mine. A freight car loaded with food was dynamited. And as white flags fluttered in the dawn the miners stormed in over the embankments surrounding the mine.

They came over the banks, cursing and yelling like Indians. Many of them were reeling drunk. First they struck at the captive steam-shovel men with their fists. Then, having tasted blood, they started to hammer some with their gun butts. Who had operated the machine gun? A goat was pointed out. The miners killed him instantly and draped his body over the machine gun.

About fifty of the men were kicked, slapped, bullied into a line, two abreast, and marched down the road to a point where there was a barbed-wire fence. McDowell, limping on his wooden leg, was beaten until he fell and could rise no more. As he lay dying, six or seven vicious Amazons in the crowd kicked him and stamped on him, and when he was dead they burned the word "scab" on his body.

The rest of the steam-shovel men were lined up in front of the barbed-wire fence and ordered to "climb the fence and run." They did. Thirteen were shot to death as they climbed. A fourteenth lived until newspapermen arrived, and died in their sight. Four died of wounds after reaching the nearby woods.

Then came a game of hare-and-hounds among the trees. The victims were given a head start and the miners came whooping in pursuit. Two of the quarry were caught and hanged to trees. Six others were tied together and dragged by an automobile along the stone road. They ran as long as they could—with great, giant, desperate strides. But as the automobile picked up speed they fell, one by one, and once they had fallen, there was no rising. They bumped and dragged along the stone road to Herrin, and there, covered with blood, their bruised and broken bodies were exhibited to the cheering populace.

Some of the mob trooped into Herrin, carrying seventeen bodies which they propped up naked in obscene poses. They tried to outdo one another in their vulgar and macabre humor. Mothers stood around with their children watching the ghastly tableau of dead men in carnal posturings.

One young woman put her foot on the breast of a dying man who begged, "Give me a drink of water before I die."

She ground her heel in his flesh and jeered, "I'll see you in hell first."

She was cheered.

The official count was twenty-six dead. Some newspapers had the toll as high as forty. No one was punished for the butchery. A grand jury found that the men had died at the hands of "persons unknown." Governor Small said he could not be held accountable because he was being tried at the time for embezzling $1,500,000 in public funds. Attorney General Brundage said he was busy prosecuting Small.

Reading the accounts, Papa Reuther said again and again, "Things like this happen when the capitalists exploit the workers."

Papa Reuther looked upon himself as a victim of capitalistic exploitation because his income was not growing as fast as his family. Something had to be done about it, and Walter, having flunked English and algebra in his first year of high school, decided he could do better in the big,

broad world. Since Herrin he had made up his mind to be
a labor leader, anyway, so he quit high school and followed
Ted into Wheeling Steel. There he became an apprentice
tool- and diemaker, unlike Ted, who was a white-collar
worker in the office.

Walter worked long days at forty cents an hour. It was
hard work for small pay, and he gagged at some plant conditions. For one thing, the men were unorganized, and
Walter, already dedicated to the future he had charted for
himself, in his boyish way tried for three years to organize
it. Remembering the debates, the folksongs, the picnics,
and other family customs, he especially rebelled against
work on Sundays and holidays. And when Columbus Day
fell on a Sunday, he organized a sit-at-home strike, a forerunner of the sitdown strike of which he would one day
make a fearsome union weapon. On Monday, when he returned to work, he was called on the carpet and fired.

Walter looked around Wheeling for work without success. Some have said his older brother Ted, having helped
him get the job at Wheeling Steel and angry at him for losing it, had refused to help him get another. Stories such as
this are almost impossible to run down, but it is interesting
to note that Ted, alone of all the Reuther brothers, has
declined having anything to do with labor agitation. He
remained with Wheeling Steel and rose to become company
paymaster.

Walter laughs about this and says, "Ted always was
the white sheep of the family."

Whatever happened, he decided there was nothing in
Wheeling for him. Detroit was then the Mecca of workmen with a mechanical bent. Since 1914, when Henry Ford
had made his then astounding offer of $5 a day, all roads
had led to the Michigan city, now the acknowledged capital

of the auto world. Georgia "crackers," Arkansas hillbillies,
Tennessee ridge runners, Alabama cotton pickers, they
swarmed in from the Deep South to earn the high wages
and taste the high life of the big city.

Reuther saw the beckoning hand, and on he went to Detroit. As one writer has remarked, "It didn't seem so at
the time, but in the labor movement his arrival in Detroit
was the equivalent of that of the young Napoleon at the
École Militaire from the cadet school at Brienne."

Young Reuther found his first job with the Briggs Manufacturing Company.

Now, if he had been quite an ordinary young fellow he
would have taken his eighty-five cents an hour, lived in a
boarding house, blown his earnings on football and baseball pools, needled beer, and floozies at two bucks a crack
when he could draw the color line and four bits for a
change of luck when he couldn't.

Even at this early period he acted like a man who knew
his destiny. He was as curiously abstemious as Adolf Hitler.
No girls, no beer, no cigarettes for him. His nearest approach to dissipation was chewing gum.

He took regular exercise. He swam and played his
favorite basketball at the Detroit YMCA. His newspaper
route had made him accustomed to walking, and when he
had finished his shift, he often set off on a long walk, late at
night, hatless as has always been his custom, and when he
got back to his room he ended the day with a cold shower.

Reuther worked briefly for Briggs, General Motors, and
the Coleman Tool and Die Company. Then, one evening,
he saw an ad in the *Free Press*. The Ford Motor Company
had discontinued the old Model T and was retooling for
its revolutionary Model A. It was advertising for veteran
tool and die workers capable of directing a group.

The nineteen-year-old redhead had never been one to hide his light under a bushel. He had trouble getting by the special cop at the gate, still more difficulty convincing the master mechanic he was a veteran tool and die man. Persuasion was his business, however; later on, Ford's right-hand man, Charles E. Sorenson, was to say, "As a spellbinder he was a wizard." The master mechanic agreed to try young Reuther for two days. He made the grade and Ford took him on as a regular at $1.10 an hour.

The hours at Ford, 3:30 in the afternoon to 1:30 in the morning, enabled Reuther to go back and pick up the dropped stitches of education. Now the man of destiny on a charted course, he whipped through high school in two years, and when his brother Victor joined him in 1930, the two entered Wayne University.

Walter now embarked on a back-breaking course of work and study. He and Vic took a small apartment near the Wayne University campus. Home from work at 1:30 A.M., he studied until 3:00 or 4:00, sometimes falling asleep with his head among his books but always awake and freshly showered for his first class at eight in the morning.

He specialized in labor and industrial problems at Wayne. As an extracurricular activity he joined the Social Problems Club and was elected its president. When an attempt was made to organize an ROTC unit, the Reuthers mounted soapboxes on the campus and spoke out against it with all the vehement military pacifism of Grandpa Jacob Reuther. They rushed to the defense of a professor suspended for his outspoken criticism of the ROTC, and at a rally for him Victor made the opening speech, and Walter, the closing. The professor was reinstated.

It was the first of many victories for the Reuthers.

Reuther,
the LID, and Brookwood

UNFORTUNATELY, in that year of Our Lord 1931, the economic bottom had fallen out. Two years before, Detroit's auto factories had employed nearly half a million workers. By 1930, a period of only twelve months, the figure had dropped to 341,000, and by 1931 it was no more than 257,000. Six out of every ten had lost their jobs. There were 211,000 on relief, and 150,000 had left the city to go back to the towns and the farms.

The city was in a turmoil of strikes and depression unrest, and Reuther knew that now was the time to get into the swim of labor agitation. At Wayne he had talked the most radical and labor-minded members of his Social Problems Club into forming a campus branch of the League for Industrial Democracy.

In 1931 the LID was very much a going organization.

It had been organized twenty-six years before on the second floor of Peck's Restaurant in New York City. Twenty-six years later, in 1957, it was given a veneer of deceiving respectability by such placid-faced revolutionaries as Norman Thomas and Chester Bowles, and would hold its 52nd annual luncheon on the Starlight Roof of New York's swanky but faded Waldorf-Astoria, in the dignified shadow cast by such conservative guests as former President Herbert Hoover and General Douglas MacArthur.

In on the 1905 founding were Clarence Darrow, Jack London, the author of *John Barleycorn* and *The Call of the Wild,* and the social-conscious novelist Upton Sinclair, as well as a young Wesleyan undergraduate named Henry W. Laidler, who was to become for half a century the LID's executive director.

The LID was Sinclair's baby. His idea was that, inasmuch as socialism—militant, fighting, revolutionary socialism —was not taught in the colleges, an organization should be formed to teach it on the campus. The result was the LID, which was called the Intercollegiate Socialist Society until the Bolshevik Revolution in Russia made anything unpopular which bore the tag of Marxist socialism. In 1921 the Intercollegiate Socialist Society became the League for Industrial Democracy.

It is a stark, revealing, and frightening thing to piece together, tile by tile, the pattern of Socialist revolution in the United States. There are not too many fragments in the design. A patient mind could soon put them together, because the number of active revolutionaries is not great.

But, though they are few in number, their influence has been far-reaching. Perhaps the most frightening part of the situation is that these men, who wrote the flaming call to arms to liberals in LID pamphlets of the early 1930s, fell into key posts in the Roosevelt and Truman administrations and, today, under the banner of high-sounding names like the Conference on Economic Progress, write the social philosophy of such groups as the Americans for Democratic Action.

Let us take just one of these LID editorialists of the early 1930s—Leon Keyserling, the man who wrote the Wagner Labor Relations Act and did Harry Truman's economic thinking for him after World War II.

When we reflect on the activities of men like Leon Keyserling, it becomes obvious to us that we have an interlocking directorate of Socialists in the United States. This directorate has been extremely successful for twenty-five years in placing Socialists in strategic posts inside and outside our government.

Leon Keyserling is a good example of this strategy. Starting as an attorney in the Agriculture Adjustment Administration, a bureau which spawned so many of our Pinkos, he went on from there to become legislative assistant to the late Senator Robert F. Wagner, for whom he wrote the Wagner Labor Relations Act. Subsequently, for twenty years, he had his feet in the public trough and his mind in a thousand schemes.

Keyserling's wife, Mary Dublin, is one of the most dedicated writers of LID literature. She signed the notorious "Open Letter to American Liberals"—an attack on the Trotskyites who questioned the validity of the Moscow purge trials.

Among the other signers was George Marshall, husband of Mary's sister Elizabeth. Under his brother's will, George Marshall became the administrator of the Robert Marshall Foundation, which provided funds for furthering Marxist doctrinaire thinking through "the education of the people of the United States of America to the necessity and desirability of the development and organization of unions of persons engaged in work or of unemployed persons, and the promotion and advancement of an economic system in the United States based on the theory of production for use and not for profit."

George Marshall supplied bail of $20,000 for Communist Gerhardt Eisler, who fled the country to Communist East Germany. As chairman of the subversive Civil Rights Congress, he directed the raising of a quarter-of-a-million-dollar defense fund for the Communist leaders convicted under the Smith Act in Judge Medina's Court. On June 5, 1950, Marshall himself was convicted of contempt of Congress and sent to jail for 90 days.

George Marshall and Mary Dublin, before her marriage to Keyserling, were active in many Communist-front organizations. When Keyserling became chairman of President Truman's Council of Economic Advisers, Mary Dublin was employed as chief of the Special Programs Branch, Bureau of Foreign and Domestic Commerce in the Department of Commerce.

She reported to Thomas C. Blaisdell, Jr., Assistant Secretary of Commerce until 1950, who himself is an interesting example of the interlocking directorate. His wife Catherine and his father were witnesses to the last will and testament of Robert Marshall establishing the foundation to promote Marxist production for use and not for profit.

From 1935 to 1939 Blaisdell was a member of the Industrial Committee of the National Resources Committee established in 1935 by President Roosevelt. His colleagues were members of the Socialist-Communist interlocking directorate—Isador Lubin, Lauchlin Currie, and Harry Dexter White.

Readers who wish to know more about the close associations of this coterie should read the book *Redirecting Education,* jointly authored by Thomas C. Blaisdell, Jr., Leon Keyserling, and Rexford G. Tugwell. Some of Keyserling's contributions, shorn of their vague verbiage, are direct and shameless attacks on capitalism.

Today Keyserling is busy turning out economic studies with a socialistic twist for the Conference on Economic Progress, of whose executive committee Walter Reuther is an active and enthusiastic member.

So, by ten times ten thousand slender red and pink threads, woven in and out of our governmental, economic, and social structure, Walter Reuther can be bound to David Dubinsky, and David Dubinsky to Leon Keyserling, and Leon Keyserling to George Marshall, and George Marshall to Harry Dexter White, and Harry Dexter White to Eleanor Roosevelt, and Eleanor Roosevelt back to Walter Reuther again.

Threads of these colors bound Walter Reuther to such institutions as Brookwood Labor College at Katonah, N.Y., whose destiny he helped to guide. Brookwood has been tagged by the American Federation of Labor as Communistic. It got $115,000 in funds from the American Fund for Public Service, whose other beneficiaries included *The Daily Worker,* the Vanguard Press, the Russian Reconstruction Farms, and the Young Communist League. When Brookwood Labor College went out of business, Walter Reuther inherited its library.

By 1932 Roy, the youngest Reuther, had joined Walter and Vic in Detroit, and all were active on the picket lines. During the strike on the picket lines at Briggs, where Walter had worked and where he now met another young firebrand named Emil Mazey, he led a whole contingent of

Wayne University students in demonstrations for the striking workers. When he wasn't on the picket lines he was haranguing any time, any place. He had the luggage compartment removed from an old coupé he owned, and a speaker's platform installed, and this gave him a mobile platform he could use whenever and wherever the occasion arose.

It was only one short step from the LID to the Socialist Party, and this step Walter and Victor took this same year of 1932, when Roosevelt was running against Hoover. Intrigued by the Socialist slogan "Repeal Unemployment," a take-off on the Democratic slogan "repeal the Eighteenth Amendment," the socialistic Reuthers worked like Trojans campaigning for Thomas.

By this time Walter, twenty-five years old, was foreman over forty tool and die workers in the Ford plant. His superiors were growing weary of his union activities, however, and now that he was openly campaigning for the Socialist Party they could endure him no more. In the midst of the "Happy Days Are Here Again" whooping and tumult that marked Roosevelt's election over Herbert Hoover, Walter Reuther opened his pay envelope and found a pink slip.

To most men a pink slip is a tragedy. To Walter Reuther it was merely a vindication of his attitude toward capitalism in general and management in particular. It was also a grand opportunity. Vic and he would take a turn about the world and study the labor movement on a global scale.

In February, 1933, luckily just before Governor W. A. Comstock anticipated Roosevelt's Bank Holiday, they withdrew their savings and left for New York. In Manhattan they had dinner with J. B. Matthews, Paul Porter, Ruth Schallcross, and Mary Hillyer, later to become the wife of the anti-Roman Catholic Paul Blanshard. All the diners were intellectuals of a liberal bent, all board members of socialism's interlocking directorates, although at least one, Matthews, would later cross to the other side of the ideological tracks and become an investigator for the House Committee on Un-American Activities and a notable critic of those who dwell on the political Left Bank.

In this cozy setting Walter Reuther confided that the real objective of their tour was the Soviet Union, where they hoped to teach as well as be taught.

The architect of the future was beginning his blueprint.

The Roving Reuthers Abroad

I_N that February of 1933, when Walter and Victor Reuther took third-class passage to Germany, Soviet Russia was in every sense "a riddle wrapped in a mystery inside an enigma."

Many left-minded young intellectuals looked to it for guidance. As a matter of fact, on the February day the Reuthers' ship docked at Bremerhaven, Harold R. Ware was homeward bound, on his chest the Order of Lenin and, in his head, plans to form the Communist cell of government workers in Washington which in time would shelter Alger Hiss and some of Felix Frankfurter's other Happy Hot Dogs.

It was months before Roosevelt would hold the cozy sessions with Maxim Litvinov which finally resulted in diplomatic recognition of the USSR. To be sure, Roosevelt, the President-elect, had not as yet taken office.

The Reuthers reached Berlin just in time to witness the Reichstag fire. The Nazis said Communist Jews had set it. The Communists said the Nazis had set it themselves. In the end the Nazis fixed the blame on a Dutch Communist named Marinus van der Lubbe and chopped off his head.

Aflame with radical ideas and eager for new experiences, Walter and Victor bought bicycles in Stuttgart, and, once in the saddle, they set out on a cycling tour which took them over large sections of Germany, France, and England. On the road they slept in haystacks, youth hostels, and the homes of young anti-Nazis, some of whom they helped to smuggle out of Germany and into Switzerland. In Mannheim, the city their grandfather had fled, they dared not raise their voices when they saw Nazis beat a young worker.

Of the countries they visited, Britain, sleeping smugly in its latter-day feudalism, was the only one in which the workers had a semblance of political power. Even there, however, the Reuthers found themselves unable to get *en rapport* with the workers as they did in Germany. Both Reuthers spoke German, and in the German youth hostels they took part in the long political discussions which were an essential part of that country's life in the 1930s. Besides, there was a feeling of conspiracy in the air which appealed to the politically adventurous souls of the Reuthers.

One night the roving Reuthers found themselves watching a propaganda film. At the end a huge swastika was flashed upon the screen. The audience stood up, gave the Heil Hitler salute, and commenced singing the Horst Wessel song.

Boldly, the Reuthers sat tight. Their red heads made them stand out, an oasis of disrespectful *sitzfleisch* in a desert of respectful Nazis. Seeing all eyes upon them, the Reuthers opened a hasty conversation in English to show they were foreigners. But the crowd was in an ugly mood, and the Reuthers got a good shoving around before the helmeted police arrived, swinging truncheons, and saved them from serious bodily injury.

When he related the experience afterward, Walter Reuther said: "After that, we were careful. We sang the workers' songs in workers' gatherings, and the Nazi songs in Nazi gatherings." Still, they managed to have narrow escapes, once by a rope ladder from a second-story window while the Gestapo searched for them in the cellar.

The Reuthers had to wait almost a year before their Russian visas came through, and they passed the time visiting mills, factories, mines. They talked with workers at every opportunity, learned all there was to be learned about industrial techniques and the trade-union movement in Germany.

As soon as their visas arrived, they sold their bikes and went by train to Moscow. It was December 1933, in a country whose government the United States had just recognized. The Russian winter had set in, and it was forty below in Moscow when the Reuthers, dressed in light clothing, stepped down from the train.

Shivering, they hurried on to Gorki, the industrial city named after Russia's famed hobo short-story writer. Walter's pocket was picked on a crowded streetcar, and they were out of funds when they arrived at their destination, which was an automobile plant built for the Russians by the Ford Motor Company.

Walter Reuther has never revealed what was his "Open sesame" to Russia. It does not seem reasonable that two American workers in their twenties, without funds, and possessed of little more than idle curiosity, could have entered Russia, the mystery of mysteries and the forever suspicious,

unless some influential person or persons prepared the way
for them. If the Reuthers did carry letters of introduction
from American Socialists or Communists, no one has
revealed whose magic name adorned the surface.

This much we do know: they were welcomed at the plant,
where they mingled with workers of many nationalities,
among them American construction workers who lived at
Amerikanski Pusholik. To Walter, a skilled tool- and die-
worker, was given the job of training oafish peasant lads in
precise machinist work. In time he became a leader of a brigade of sixteen workers and won bonuses for his production
ideas.

A Russian hand worker in fact, he did not forget that he
was also a brain worker, and in his spare time he wrote articles for Moscow's English-language newspaper on methods to
improve production.

Most of that writing has been lost to posterity, but, about
a month after their arrival in Gorki, the Reuthers penned a
letter to their fellow worker Melvin Bishop and his wife
Gladys. The letter, signed "Vic and Wal" but probably written by Victor, has become a controversial item in the lives of
the Reuther boys. The Reuthers have claimed that parts of
the letter are forged, without specifying which parts, other
than the closing sentence. Still, there is little doubt that a
letter was written from Russia, and this is the version of it
read into the Congressional Record.

January 21, 1934

Dear Mel and Glad: Your letter of December 5 arrived
here last week from Germany and was read with more
than usual interest by Wal and I. It seemed ages since we
had heard from you, so you might well imagine with what
joy we welcomed news from Detroit. It is precisely be-

cause you are equally anxious, I know, to receive word from the "workers' fatherland" that I am taking this opportunity to answer you.

What you have written concerning the strikes and the general labor unrest in Detroit plus what we have learned from other sources of the rising discontent of the American workers, makes us long for the moment to be back with you in the front lines of the struggle; however, the daily inspiration that is ours as we work side by side with our Russian comrades in our factory, the thought that we are actually helping to build a society that will forever end the exploitation of man by man, the thought that what we are building will be for the benefit and enjoyment of the working class, not only of Russia, but for the entire world, is the compensation we receive for our temporary absence from the struggle in the United States. And let no one tell you that we are not on the road to socialism in the Soviet Union. Let no one say that the workers of the Union of Soviet Socialist Republics are not on the road to security, enlightenment, and happiness.

Mel, you know Wal and I were always strong for the Soviet Union. You know we were always ready to defend it against the lies of reactionaries. But let me tell you, now that we are here seeing all the great construction, watching a backward peasantry being transformed into an enlightened, democratic, cultured people, now that we have already experienced the thrill, the satisfaction of participating in genuine proletarian democracy, we are more than just sympathetic toward our country, we are ready to fight for it and its ideals. And why not? Here the workers, through their militant leadership, the proletarian dictatorship, have not sold out to the owning class like the S.P. in Germany and like the Labor Party in

England. Here they have against all odds, against famine, against internal strife and civil war, against sabotage, against capitalist invasion and isolation, our comrades here have maintained power, they have won over the masses, they have transformed the "dark masses" of Russia into energetic, enlightened workers. They have transformed the Soviet Union into one of the greatest industrial nations of the world. They have laid the economic foundation for socialism, for a classless society. Mel, if you could be with us for just one day in our shop meeting and watch the workers as they offer suggestions and constructive criticism of production in the shop. Here are no bosses to drive fear into the workers. No one to drive them in mad speedups. Here the workers are in control. Even the shop superintendent has no more right in these meetings than any other worker. I have witnessed many times already when the superintendent spoke too long, the workers in the hall decided he had already consumed enough time and the floor was then given to a lathe hand who told of his problems and offered suggestions. Imagine this at Ford or Briggs. This is what the outside world calls the "ruthless dictatorship" in Russia. I tell you, Mel, in all the countries we have thus far been in, we have never found such genuine proletarian democracy. It is unpolished and crude, rough and rude, but proletarian workers' democracy in every respect. The workers in England have more culture and polish when they speak at their meetings but they have no power. I prefer the latter.

In our factory, which is the largest and most modern in Europe, and we have seen them all, there are no pictures of Fords and Rockefellers, of Roosevelts and Mellon. No such parasites, but rather huge pictures of Lenin, * * * etc., greet the workers' eyes on every side. Red

banners with slogans "Workers of the World Unite," are
draped across the craneways. Little red flags fly from the
tops of the presses, drill presses, lathe kells, etc. Such a
sight you have never seen before. Women and men work
side by side—the women with their red cloth about their
heads, 5 days per week (our week here is 6 days long).
At noon we all eat in a large factory restaurant where
wholesome plain food is served. A workers' band furnishes
music to us from an adjoining room while we have dinner.
For the remainder of our 1-hour lunch period we adjourn
to the "red" corner recreation, where workers play games,
read papers and magazines or technical books, or merely
sit, smoke and chat. Such a fine spirit of comradeship you
have never before witnessed in your life. Superintendent
leaders and ordinary workers are all alike. If you saw our
superintendent as he walks through the shop greeting
workers with, "Hello, comrade," you could not distin-
guish him from any other worker.

The interesting thing, Mel, is that 3 years ago this
place here was a vast prairie, a waste land, and the thousands of workers here who are building complicated dies
and other tools were at that time peasants who had never
before even seen an industry let alone worked in one.
And by mere brute determination, by the determination
to build a workers' country second to none in the world;
urged on by the spirit of the revolution, they have con-
structed this huge marvelous auto factory which is today
turning out modern cars for the Soviet Union. Through
the bitter Russian winters of 45° below they have toiled
with their bare hands, digging foundations, erecting struc-
tures; they have with their own brute strength pulled the
huge presses into place and set them up for operation.
What they have here they have sacrificed and suffered for;

that is why they are not so ready to turn it all over again to the capitalists. That is why today they still have comrades from the "red army" on guard at the factory at all times to prevent counter-revolutionaryists from carrying on their sabotage.

About a 20-minute walk from the factory an entirely new Socialist city has grown up in these 3 years. Here over 50,000 of the factory workers live in fine, new modern, apartment buildings. Large hospitals, schools, libraries, theaters, and clubs have sprung up here, and all for the use of those who work, for without a worker's card one cannot make use of all these modern facilities. Three nights ago we were invited to the clubhouse in Sosgow (Socialist city) to attend an evening of enjoyment given by the workers of the die shop. Imagine, all the workers with whom we daily work came together that evening for a fine banquet, a stage performance, a concert, speeches, and a big dance. A division of the "red" army was also present as guests. In all my life, Mel, I have never seen anything so inspiring. Mel, once a fellow has seen what is possible where workers gain power, he no longer fights just for an ideal, he fights for something which is real, something tangible. Imagine, Mel, Henry Ford throwing a big party for his slaves. Here the party was no gift of charity from someone above for we own the factory, we held the meeting, and decided to have the party, and it was paid for from the surplus earnings of our department. What our department does is typical of the social activities which are being fostered throughout the entire factory and the entire Soviet Union.

Mel, we are witnessing and experiencing great things in the U.S.S.R. We are seeing the most backward nation in the world being rapidly transformed into the most

modern and scientific with new concepts and new social
ideals coming into force. We are watching daily socialism
being taken down from the books on the shelves and put
into actual application. Who could not be inspired by
such events?

And now my letter is getting long and still I have said
little, for there is so much to say and so little time in
which to do it. We have written Merlin and Coach rather
lengthy letters and have requested they forward them to
you to save duplicity of material.

I believe there is little in this letter which they have
not already received so there will be no need of your
forwarding this to them.

A word about your letter. * * *

Keep your eye on the S.P. It being affiliated to the
Second International, I am not so certain it is "drifting"
in the right direction, certainly not in the light of recent
events.

Let us know definitely what is happening to the
Y.P.S.L. and also the "Social Problems" Club at C.C.C.
* * *

Carry on the fight for a Soviet America.

Vic and Wal

Is the letter genuine? That is a moot question.

The Reuthers do not deny that Victor wrote the Bishops
one or more letters praising the Russian struggle for economic
improvement. Walter says this particular one was written in
"a burst of adolescent enthusiasm." If he is speaking of his
own emotions, he was twenty-six, somewhat old for an adolescent. He goes on to describe the version circulated as distorted, and declares the closing sentence a libelous forgery.

During the NLRB hearings in Detroit, on July 8, 1937,

questioned by Louis J. Colombo of Ford's legal staff, he denied authorship of the letter, which could be technically true, because actual authorship is usually attributed to Victor.

On October 13, 1938, when the House Committee on Un-American Activities held a hearing in Detroit, a witness, Herman Luhrs, of Flint, chairman of the American Legion's Committee on Subversion, read the text into the record. Luhrs said his copy had been made on the typewriter by Roy Reuther, who is referred to as Coach in the context. Luhrs swore to its authenticity.

The letter was mailed in Abmozazoff, Topkini, Russia, the witness said, and the letter bore this return address: Victor G. Reuther, B. Paumep, Anepikarakin, II, Don. 4. Representative E. E. Cox of Georgia, who has called Walter Reuther "as violent a Red as was ever turned loose on the American public by Russian communism," later read the letter into the Congressional Record.

Although declaring the public text distorted, neither brother has attempted to restore the original text. Neither has indicated which parts are genuine, which spurious, except for the ending.

At the CIO convention in Boston in 1942, Melvin Bishop, then estranged from Reuther, said Reuther could deny the validity of the letter if he wished to do so, but he, Bishop, knew better, for he was the one who had received it.

In 1948, Victor wrote to the *Saturday Evening Post,* which was to publish excerpts from the letter: "I confess I was somewhat surprised to learn that significance is still being placed on 'that letter,' despite the public record which Walter has built on this subject during the past fifteen years. I appreciate the fact, however, that the readers of the *Post* are entitled to know the facts. . . .

"No one who is at all familiar with my style of writing would recognize any similarity between the text of this letter, a copy of which you forwarded to me, and the way in which I wrote then or write now."

Walter Reuther would long remember his experiences in Europe. Years later he would tell of standing on a hill overlooking the city of Esslingen near Stuttgart, in May 1933. There were about five hundred Storm Troopers in Nazi uniform around a tremendous bonfire. The Storm Troopers had just planted what they called the Hitler Eiche—the Hitler Oak—next to the Bismarck Oak. After speeches by their leaders the Storm Troopers cast into the bonfire first the flag of the German Republic and then the flag of the German trade-union movement.

"I stood near a union brother in plain clothes," Walter Reuther said later in describing the scene. "He was a shop steward in one of the manufacturing plants in Esslingen. He was a member of the trade-union movement, the German Metal Trades Union. He had marched behind that trade-union flag. It symbolized all the hopes and aspirations and security for which he had struggled.

"And when the German leader of the Nazi Storm Troopers cast that flag into the fire and said the destruction of these two flags, the flag of the German Republic and the flag of the German trade-union movement, symbolized the complete destruction of the 'Old Order,' and 'upon these ashes we shall build the Nazi Third Reich,' this young trade-union brother could no longer refrain from open expression of his hatred and determination to fight against this Nazi tyranny. As the trade-union flag was thrown into the fire, he cried out, '*Das hast du gestohlen*—You have stolen that flag.'

"For merely saying that, he was pounced upon by about thirty Storm Troopers, and I saw him beaten into unconsciousness before my eyes.

"When I left that community some three weeks later our brother the shop steward in the German Metal Trades Union was dead, at only twenty-two. He had been executed because he dared raise his voice against the brutal gangsterism of Hitler. His younger brother of only eighteen, who had vainly come to his assistance, was still in a concentration camp."

After a year at Gorki, the Reuthers took a train across the Siberian wastes to Harbin, spent a few weeks in China, looked in on India's movement for national independence, passed two months in Japan, where they expressed themselves as shocked at the growth of militarism, and finally signed on a freighter as deck hands. They worked their way across the Pacific, an adventure which the hiring halls of the Maritime Union now deny to enterprising young men.

It has been written that no one could have asked for a more direct education in modern realities. No one was to need it more than the young man about to lead the largest union in America. With his brother Victor, he had felt the social and political bumps on the world's surface. If, in the future, he should fail to measure up to his responsibilities, he could hardly plead ignorance. He had had history thrust into his face. He had seen blood shed. From that time on he would be as young as today and as old as his grandfathers.

Bosses Don't Care About People

I<small>N</small> the fall of 1935 Walter Reuther came home from Russia with two convictions. First of all, God wasn't as important to him as people, and, secondly, people weren't important to bosses at all.

No sooner was Reuther home than he got back to riding the circuit for labor. He had always been an active hitchhiker. You might even say he had hitchhiked and mooched his way around the world. But, then, hitchhiking was one way of getting about at little expense, and with the help of his hooked thumb, Reuther toured the Midwest, attending labor, young people's, and radical meetings and conventions as far south as Arkansas.

It wasn't very long after his return that Walter and his two brothers Victor and Roy helped to conduct a conference in Columbus, Ohio, at which the Communist National Students League and the Socialist Student League for Industrial Democracy were merged into the American Student Union.

Now, if there's anything Walter Reuther is sensitive about, it's his bad right arm. He squeezed that rubber ball hour after hour, day after day, and took up woodworking as a hobby to restore the strength in his arm. But the hurt was deep. The shotgun pellets smashed his right elbow and frayed the nerves, and it's a wonder that doctors were able to save the limb at all. He can't shake hands with his old abandon. It's a definite handicap.

If Reuther's crippled righthandedness is one sore spot, his political lefthandedness is another. He insists to high heaven he never was a Communist. A Socialist, yes, but never a Communist, and he probably never was, in the technical sense. Like John L. Lewis, he was above communism. A political Archimedes, he merely used it to move the social world.

During this period he was known as an active worker for radical causes. At the Columbus convention the representative of the Communist Party's central committee, Celeste Strack, vouched for the brothers Reuther as men of the right stripe—the right stripe being an ideological bar sinister. Walter and Victor represented Brookwood Labor College, which has taken full credit for the organization of the UAW. Roy registered as a representative of Wayne University, where Walter had organized the LID. Later on, Walter would help Anna Louise Strong, editor of the Moscow *Daily News,* to collect money for the Spanish Loyalists.

In 1936 Victor taught at the Southern Workers Anti-War Summer School at Commonwealth College in Mena, Arkansas. Authorities convicted this school under an Arkansas statute on charges of anarchy, of failure to display the American flag, and of flying instead the hammer-and-sickle emblem of Communist Russia.

In that same year, on March 18, the Young People's Socialist League held a meeting at the Masonic Temple in Flint. A labor amazon named Nordine Johnson introduced Reuther, who spoke to the "Yipsols" on the topic, "Russia's Economic Position Today."

It was quite a speech, embroidered by Reuther with tales of derring-do from his European adventures. He boasted that the Nazis had made things hot for him in Germany and told of escaping by a second-story window, down a rope, when the Gestapo came for him at his grandmother's house. In Japan, however, he had no rope trick to save himself, and was forced to fall back on his American citizenship.

In his talk, Reuther went to great lengths to explain the Russian attitude toward factory life. The workers, he said, elect their own foremen and superintendents. They do the hiring and the firing by ballot, and they set their own speed of production. This speech was significant. If reported correctly, it was a carbon copy of the controversial letter Vic and Wal had sent to Mel and Gladys Bishop.

A question period followed the Reuther talk, and someone in the audience arose and asked:

"Do you believe in religion and God or in science as a religion?"

Reuther's answer was:

"We do not believe in God, but that Man is God."

Soon after coming home, Reuther went back to the labor wars. Labor organizing was still a tough racket. Perhaps it was not quite as tough as it had been back in the 1920s, when the automotive industry was a law unto itself.

Layoffs had always been part and parcel of the industrial pattern. When Ford discontinued production of the model T and started retooling for the model A in May, 1927, 100,000 men were laid off—60,000 in Detroit area alone. All of them were out of work for six months, and many of them had no job for a full year.

The fear of unemployment that dogged the auto worker's life became permanent with the depression. The memory of those dog days would leave lasting scars. Fear ate into the tissue of their lives. They were afraid to join unions. They feared to talk to one another. If a man spoke out of turn, a foreman might take him to the window, point to the knot of sorry-looking men at the employment gate and say, "If you don't like your job there's plenty on the outside looking in."

Labor was restive. As Leon Henderson said, "Labor unrest exists to a degree higher than warranted by the depression. The unrest flows from insecurity, low annual earnings, inequitable hiring and rehiring methods, espionage, speedup and displacement of workers at an extremely early age. Unless something is done soon, the workers intend to take things into their own hands and get results."

Not too many paid heed to Henderson. He was looked upon as a New Deal busybody. One of the poems current at the time went like this:

> *There goes Leon,*
> *Glowing like a neon,*
> *He's got an appointment*
> *In somebody's ointment.*

The fact was that few realized the far-reaching changes which were taking place. As Garet Garrett has written,

"There are those who still think they are holding the pass against a revolution that may be coming up the road. But they are gazing in the wrong direction. The revolution is behind them. It went by in the Night of Depression, singing songs to freedom."

Walter Reuther was a part of that revolution. It has been said that, since the destruction of chattel slavery and the triumph of the capitalist economy, the most important change in the United States was the emergence of mass industrial unions. No one has done more than Walter Reuther to help them emerge.

The old policy of the American Federation of Labor under Gompers had been to win work benefits by legislative means, by "pure and simple unionism" tactics, and from the time Teddy Roosevelt took office Gompers made progress. There were strikes under Gompers, to be sure. There were strikes and bloody fighting under John L. Lewis. But not even the bloodiest strikes had posed the question of property rights versus labor rights as pointedly as it was posed in the late fall and early winter of 1935 under the new, young, aggressive, Socialist-minded labor leaders who led the revolution "coming up the road."

Property rights have always been sacred in America. There is hardly a schoolboy who is not familiar with the guarantees of "life, liberty and the pursuit of happiness." In the original Declaration and Resolves of the First Continental Congress, October 14, 1774, these guarantees were "life, liberty and property."

Property rights were inviolable right down to the time of the trial of Bruno Richard Hauptmann for the death of the Lindbergh baby, not during a kidnaping, but in connection with the theft of a sleeping garment during the burglary of a private dwelling in the nighttime. So read the indictment upon which Hauptmann went to the electric chair.

To safeguard their sacred property, in case of the failure of the local constabulary, industry hired private police. It was an industrial practice that had been going on for more than half a century. The traditional source of security police was the Pinkerton Detective Agency, to which General Motors paid a $419,000 retainer as late as 1935. Chrysler had its own battalions under the guidon of the Corporation Auxiliaries Corporation. And Ford had Harry Bennett.

Another turn in the tide that benefited labor organizers was the election of Franklin D. Roosevelt. The model he had adopted was his distant cousin Teddy, the man who had once evoked Franklin Delano's astonishment for the high-handed methods he had used in settling the steel strike a generation before.

The National Industrial Recovery Act in 1933 was not the only shot of adrenalin the Administration gave the labor movement. From various Washington agencies the unions got such Russian-trained spokesmen as Lee Pressman, a Communist attorney who would mastermind the CIO through its most critical months.

The younger and more radical of the labor leaders had always been a little critical of the American Federation of Labor, which had been primarily a union of skilled workers, and in 1935 Lewis was ready to bolt the AFL and go over to the Congress of Industrial Organizations and, under the slogan of "Organize the Unorganized," which is heard to this day, to build up a mass industrial union.

With Lewis went the youngsters in the labor movement: thirty-year-old Lee Pressman, twenty-nine-year-old Reuther and Bob Travis, and twenty-five-year-old James Carey.

From such sources as Whittaker Chambers' *Witness* and Lee Pressman's cathartic testimony before the House Committee on Un-American Activities in 1950, we know that Fifth Amendment Communists like Edwin S. Smith, Nathan Witt, and Charles Kramer moved from the Agricultural Adjustment Administration to other governmental agencies, including the Red-ridden National Labor Relations Board, where Smith was a board member from 1934 to 1941, Witt was secretary from 1927 to 1940, and Kramer was a staff member from 1938 to 1942. This made it cozy, indeed, for Pressman, who was general counsel of the CIO during the same period.

On May 21, 1953, Smith, a member of the faculty at exclusive Putney School in Vermont, went down to Washington and invoked the Fifth Amendment when he was asked if he had been a Communist over a period from 1930, when he was Commissioner of Labor and Industries in Massachusetts, down to the day of his testimony. After he left the NLRB, Smith became a registered agent of Sovfoto, handling photographs from the Soviet Union. As an agent for Eastfoto, he distributed the photos which tried to show the United States engaged in germ warfare during the Korean war.

The new young labor leaders called the American Federation of Labor old-womanish. They called Section 7a of the NRA the Magna Carta of Labor, but they wanted more, so they went out and bought more power for labor from Franklin Roosevelt, the President of the United States.

Lewis has talked rather freely about the deal, although our free press has not passed on too much of the story to the American public.

"The United Mine Workers and the CIO have paid cash on the barrel for every piece of legislation that we have gotten," Lewis told his biographer, Saul Alinsky. ". . . Is anyone fool enough to believe for one instant that we gave this money to Roosevelt because we were spellbound by his voice? It is common knowledge that we spent approximately three quarters of a million dollars in the 1936 campaign. And you might be interested to know that the $500,000 direct contribution wasn't my price, but was the figure named by the White House, and I was given approximately forty-eight hours to get that money. Certainly there was a quid pro quo—the right for labor to organize."

Lewis, doing business on both sides of the street, had trouble with a faction of the CIO the same year he bought the Wagner Labor Act from Roosevelt for a cool half million. Needled by the Communists and the Socialists, some labor leaders raised protests against supporting Roosevelt. The result was that Lewis, having invested half a million in Roosevelt, had to buy CIO support of him for $100,000.

With the right to organize clinched, and a little pin money from Lewis to carry on an organization campaign, CIO leaders needed only a strike weapon that would get them past the locked gates and the armed guards protecting not the company property alone but the men who resisted union persuasion for one reason or another.

They found the weapon in the sitdown strike, and its greatest exponent was Walter Reuther. He can't be called the father of the sitdown. The tactic is probably as old as the master-servant relationship, and the actual words "sit down" can be found in a papyrus record of Roman Egypt in the second century, when there was labor trouble in an alabaster quarry. One gang refused to be assigned to a difficult part of the quarry.

Their foreman reported their complaint to his superior in these words:

"Some of the men came to me and said, 'We are going out to our old place and sit down until you bring us word.'"

They won the sitdown and were reassigned to their original location.

The only record of labor trouble in ancient Italy tells of a dispute that arose after the Emperor Aurelian found evidence of graft in the old Roman mint and ordered it closed. The workmen, like modern sitdowners, fortified themselves in the building, and the Emperor, unlike some contemporary governors, had to call up troops to drive them out.

In recent years the French were the first to lead with their buttocks. But, if Reuther wasn't the father, at least he was the foster father, and in his hands the *derrière* became something more than a weapon of passive resistance.

In France, Communists had inspired the sitdowns and on this side of the Atlantic they were in the forefront of the movement from the first squat. Once started, the sitdowns spread like wildfire. By force and violence, strikers took over factory after factory, welding shut the gates and doors and destroying or damaging finished products, raw materials, and in many cases valuable machinery.

By 1936, when Walter Reuther was twenty-nine, he had learned certain definite things about himself. One was that he wanted power, and another was that he had a natural gift for leading men.

In those days the UAW was a pretty ineffectual organization. When Reuther joined West Side Local No. 174, it consisted of a handful of members. For instance, when a meeting was called to elect a delegate to the UAW national convention in South Bend, Indiana, Walter and only seven others put in an appearance. Walter Reuther was by far the most enthusiastic one present, so he was named delegate.

The union treasury, which consisted of one five-dollar bill, was turned over to him, and he wrapped it around a couple of dollars he had in his own pocket. Hatless, boyish, and an "undissipated-looking Prince of Wales," as someone called him, he went from the meeting out into the street and started walking east and hooking his thumb, for, if he was going to get to South Bend, he had to hitchhike his way.

That South Bend convention was a landmark for Walter Reuther—and the UAW. Reuther, with his socialistic dialectic, had only to make a single speech to get himself elected to the UAW's international executive council, and the executive council had to take only one vote to break away from the do-nothing AFL with its principles of craft unionism and join the free-swinging CIO under two-fisted John L. Lewis.

In South Bend, Reuther shared a hotel room with five other delegates. They took turns sleeping on the bed, and as long as they had any money they ate hamburgers. By the time the convention was over, Reuther's money was gone and his belt was drawn tight, but, filled with enthusiasm, he started hitchhiking his way back to Detroit. Now they had something to fight for and with, and Walter Reuther and the UAW were going places.

With funds he borrowed from a friend, he set up an office at Twenty-fourth and Michigan. He bought a second-hand desk, rented a battered typewriter and a mimeograph machine, and began making strong speeches, running off handbills and distributing them at factory gates. He worked like a Trojan, and the pay-off was slow in coming, because fear of management reprisal was strong in the hearts of the workers.

To succeed, he must do something big and dramatic.

In South Bend, during November, workers had taken a cue from the French and attacked with the buttocks. Reuther looked about him for a place where he might stage a sitdown strike, and his gaze lighted on the Kelsey-Hayes plant, which employed 5,000 to make brakes for the Ford Company. There had been a recent speedup there, and some of the workers were disgruntled.

He held a strategy meeting at his home. Many of Local No. 174's members worked at Kelsey-Hayes. But, of the seventy-eight members, only fifteen showed up at the strategy session. Almost all fifteen worked on the brake-assembly line, the section of the plant most affected by the speedup.

Reuther found his dramatic incident. He tells of it in these words: "We had a big Polish gal at the meeting who had fainted on the assembly line once before. We assigned her to 'faint' again, and showed her how to do it. That was to be the signal. When she 'fainted,' someone else was to shut down the assembly line. We trained a couple of men in pulling the right switches."

Victor Reuther had obtained a job on the floor below the brake-assembly line. Next day, when the Polish gal fainted, two men pulled the switches and stopped the assembly line, and those in on the plot shouted, "Strike! Strike!" Victor ran upstairs, leaped onto a packing crate, and harangued the workers with an organizing speech.

Attracted by the uproar, workmen streamed in from other sections of the factory. The personnel manager stormed in, tugged at Victor's pants leg and told him to order the men back to work.

"Walter Reuther's the only one can get them to go back to work," Victor said.

"Who is Walter Reuther?" asked the personnel manager.

Victor identified his brother, and the personnel manager called him on the phone. Walter was waiting for the call, and when it came, he told the personnel manager he would try to get the men to go back to work, but could undertake it only if permitted to enter the plant.

This seemed to the personnel manager a small concession. He sent a company car for Reuther, who found the brake division jammed with wondering workers, for by this time the entire plant was idle in the excitement and confusion.

Walter took Victor's place on the packing box and told the workers the advantages of joining the union.

All the time he was talking the personnel manager pulled his leg. "Can't you get them to go back to work?" he asked.

"Can't get them back till they're organized," Reuther replied, and all the time Victor and the others were passing out hundreds of application blanks and getting them signed.

Next morning, workers reporting at the gate found the plant closed. Reuther had anticipated this. He told the workers to follow him, picked out a window that had been purposely left unlocked, and climbed in. The workers climbed in behind him and sat down. Then Reuther climbed out and organized a food supply system. It took but five days to break the back of management opposition. Faced with something new, which it could not fight, management gave in, recognized the UAW as bargaining agent, and granted a pay hike.

It was the first triumph for the auto workers by means of Lenin's strategic minority. They hailed Reuther as a brilliant tactician, and memberships poured into Local No. 174.

It had started with seventy-eight, and in a few weeks it claimed 30,000.

On that tidal wave of membership applications, Reuther began his ride to national prominence.

All Hell Breaks Loose

WALTER REUTHER now found himself in the center of the industrial stage, with the curtain going up on one of the great social dramas of our age.

It was a tragicomical drama that played forty-four days and nights to a world audience. Its title was "They Sit to Conquer."

The *dramatis personae* comprised:

General Motors Corporation, king of the automotive world, and William Knudsen and Alfred P. Sloan, its crown princes.

The CIO and the UAW, with beetle-browed John L. Lewis president of the first, and beetle-brained Homer Martin, reformed minister, president of the second.

Governor Frank Murphy, most monastic looking of all villains.

The President of the United States, saddlesore from riding the fence, and his hand-wringing Secretary of Labor, Mrs. Frances "Ma" Perkins.

The sitdown strikers, the National Guard, judges, city officials and police, politicians, an alarmed press, and hundreds of extras armed with blackjacks, brickbats, clubs, and other weapons for mob scenes.

The plot was simple. General Motors Corporation holds the mortgage on the homestead and wants to dispossess the sitdown strikers. The local sheriff is to do the dirty work. In the nick of time a knight in shining armor comes riding up. Only at this point the plot becomes confused. Ma Perkins wrings her handkerchief. John L. Lewis glowers. Everyone issues statements. Courts hand down decisions but no one pays any attention to them. The National Guard marches and countermarches. Across the city of Flint the rioting ebbs and flows with hardly any hindrance. The chief of police is driven from the city, down the Dixie Highway with siren screaming. All the extras in the mob scenes lay about them freely with baseball bats. The result is complete and utter confusion, except that somehow Walter Reuther emerges triumphant. Probably not even he knows how or why.

Such is the plot of the play "They Sit to Conquer."

After Reuther's signal victory at Kelsey-Hayes, there was a tidal wave of sitdown strikes. Once disgruntled workers caught the spark, it wasn't hard to keep the chain reaction going. Walter Reuther's West Side Local lined up scores of plants in the next five or six months.

Reuther has given an idea of how spontaneous it was. He has said, "A guy we never heard of would call up and say, 'We shut down such-and-such a plant. Send us over some coffee and doughnuts." So we'd send over the stuff.

Later on, we'd organize central kitchens and mobile feeding units. Our organizing committee was in session continu-
ously. We slept hardly at all. That's how we grew. It was a
real industrial revolution."

Reuther's language is conservative. It was civil war.

First, a picture of Flint. It was a city of more than
150,000. Of the more than 50,000 workers in the Fisher
Body and Chevrolet plants, fewer than 20 belonged to the
UAW.

Flint had been the birthplace of the Buick Company.
Labor bosses said General Motors owned the city body and
soul, that the newspaper and radio station carried out
General Motors' bidding. They said police, politicians,
judges did bend the knee to Knudsen and Sloan. They said
General Motors did control ministers and priests. But, if
true, after the day Roy Reuther and Bob Travis went
into Flint with the message of the great enlightenment, all
that was to be changed. First there would be fighting, heart-
break, and bloodletting for weeks. And when it was over,
Flint would belong to General Motors no longer. From
that time on it would belong in large measure to Walter
Reuther.

The first messiah of the new faith to appear in Flint
was redheaded Roy Reuther, who talked so like a Dutch
uncle to the 106 bus drivers of the Flint Trolley Coach
Company that on December 8, 1936, they sat down on the
job. Like a small bonfire in the forest that gets out of control, the flames caught and spread until they engulfed the
Fisher Body and Chevrolet plants.

It is hard to picture the swirling, brawling mob scenes
that were to come. For the first few days after workers began taking over the plants there was quiet—the quiet of frus-
tration, the quiet before the storm. General Motors refused

to negotiate until the sitdowners got up and got out. They went on sitting obstinately.

Here and there in the lull was an isolated incident intimating what was to come, as when storekeepers reported that groups of men were visiting them and demanding financial aid or food for the strikers. Some of the storekeepers were told, "If you don't come through, you'll come down here some morning and find all your windows smashed."

Overall, there was no violence, however, until January 6, when disorder erupted in front of the Chevrolet plant at West Kearsley and Asylum Streets. Roy Reuther and William Carney, another UAW agitator, had a loud-speaker set up. Workers objected to the down-to-earth language they were using. Fighting broke out and several were hurt before a squad of police broke it up and took off Roy Slee of Toledo, O., and Harold Hubbard, a striker at the Fisher Body plant.

The Reuthers immediately organized a jail release. Exhorted by them, the mob swarmed down to the police station and blocked the street with trucks and cars. The police finally managed to disperse them with tear gas, and as the mob retreated, one man was run over and killed by an automobile.

The real bloodletting came five days later, on the night of January 11, when thirty or more were shot, beaten, and gassed in the rioting that swirled about the Fisher Body and Chevrolet plants on Chevrolet Avenue.

It was touched off when Victor Reuther rode up in a sound truck, followed by a convoy of automobiles. Victor called out to the sitdown strikers inside the plant, "Storm the gates." He called out to the pickets outside the plant, "Storm the gates." The Fisher Body plant gates had remained in the possession of plant-protection men who, although outnumbered twenty to one, defended them gallantly against the two-pronged attack. Overwhelmed, the little garrison lost the gates in the first rush. Police came up and supported the plant-protection men in a counterattack, using tear gas.

The unionists, wearing red berets or UAW overseas caps, played two firehoses from the rooftop. They hurled down nuts and bolts from their plant fortress. In the fighting outside, UAW men designated with strips of white adhesive tape on their arms swung long clubs and blackjacks made of metal rods encased in leather.

All three Reuthers were now on hand. The redheads shouted encouragement, directed the strategy of the fighting, climbed in and out of windows to direct defense and attack. Surrounded by a hard core of tough goons, Victor Reuther screamed defiance from the sound truck.

"Go home and get your guns," he shouted once, and later he yelled, "If one more person is hurt—if there is one more bit of bloodshed—you men inside the plant destroy every piece of machinery in the factory."

The fighting swelled in tempo. Down from the rooftop rained nuts and bolts, hinges and pieces of iron. The arms with the white adhesive tape swung. Clubs were falling everywhere. Bottles flew. Curbstones and bricks arched through the air. The sheriff's car and three police cruisers were overturned and wrecked. Hardly a window in the plant remained unbroken. Men staggered away holding their cut and bruised heads. Others lay still on the ground.

The Reuthers rushed here and there, like redheaded druids, wildly urging on the men to greater activity.

"Don't give up, keep on fighting," one shouted.

"Reinforcements are coming from Toledo and Akron," another yelled.

Victor scolded the police trying to fight their way to his sound truck. "You murderers," he yelled. "You better get out of here before Governor Murphy gets you."

With bloody heads, police retreated from the plant, leaving it entirely in the hands of the strikers. Governor Murphy arrived in Flint the next day and ordered out the National Guard. It came none too soon. There was bitter resentment in Flint. The citizens were in an ugly mood; the UAW men, the vast majority of them outsiders, had been able to take over their city and force their will on its inhabitants.

Maybe, now, the Governor would do something. Hope springs eternal in the human breast.

Only an estimated 2,000 of the city's 40,000 workers were taking an active part in the strike, and thousands forced into idleness had no sympathy with the walkout. By the thousands they signed cards and petitions demanding the right to go back to work. There was talk of evicting the strikers by force, and one group of workers went to *The Flint Journal* and told the editors: "We are fed up with this situation. We can't get any help from the city or from the state. We demand the right to work and we intend to see that we get that right. We have talked this thing over and have decided to act. We have about 2,500 men at Buick ready to march on the South End Fisher plant and throw those guys out with our bare hands. We don't need guns or clubs to do it, either."

Workers held secret meetings late at night. They armed themselves with whatever weapons came to hand, and as the feeling of bitterness and resentment rose, Flint came swiftly to the brink of civil war.

The direct result of this countermove was the formation of the Flint Alliance. Formed by workers and their families, it aimed at being "a rallying point for those who want to work and who want industrial peace in Flint." The workers said, "We resent the prospect of prolonged idleness and the suffering it means for ourselves and our families just when we are getting back on our feet after the years of the depression."

After the bloody riot of January 11, 4,000 workers from Buick, Chevrolet, and Fisher Body met, condemned outside strike agitation, and went on record against violence of any kind. On January 26, 8,000 jammed the I.M.A. Auditorium and another 2,500 were turned away. Those attending the rally criticized outside strike leaders and demanded the right to work. Four delegates from the meeting called on Governor Murphy and asked, "Will you guarantee all workers full protection in going to and from work?"

Murphy refused to give any such guarantee and condemned the Flint Alliance as an organization of lawlessness.

The Flint record is a pathetic one to read today. Federal troops had been called out for lesser disturbances as far back as the railroad strikes of 1877. They had restored order at the Coeur d'Alene mines in Idaho twice, in 1892 and 1899, during the Pullman strike of 1894, during other mine strikes as recently as 1921, in the steel strike of 1919, in the Seattle general strike of the same year, and in the Denver streetcar strike of 1920.

With 2,500 National Guardsmen standing by in Flint, the rioting only became more turbulent. On February 1, in a concerted action, UAW mobs attacked Chevrolet plants 4, 6, and 9 as the workers were changing shifts at 3:30 P.M. At a prearranged signal scores of women, wearing red berets and armbands marked E. B., for Emergency Brigade, rushed up with long poles and smashed all the windows in the Kearsley Street side of plant 9.

Inside 9 a knock-down, drag-out fight was going on, and nonstrikers hurled several unionists out of the building until the UAW counterattacked, using tear gas, and regained possession. Plant 4 held out so stubbornly that unionists, once they had gained control of it, ripped telephone lines from the wall and smashed all the windows.

At the height of the disturbance the fighting boiled all the way to Lansing, the state capital, which a UAW mob tried to take over. They might have succeeded if the students had not swarmed out of Michigan State University and met them in a pitched battle. The long fight ended in Lansing with many of the UAW sympathizers winding up in the lake.

There is a story that Walter Reuther once was telling a writer all the things he had to consider during the ebb and flow of battle across Flint. Reuther went into great detail concerning how UAW men had taken over a particular plant, how they had thrown up barricades to halt police, and how they collected missiles and connected a fire hose to drive off attackers.

"What if the city had shut off the water?" the friend asked.

"They couldn't have done that," Reuther is said to have protested vehemently. "That would have been against the law."

When casualties began to mount around plants 4, 6, and 9, the National Guardsmen came up and cleared the area, but made no effort to remove the sitdowners inside the plants.

Flint had now lost all semblance of law and order. Thugs openly assaulted pedestrians on the street while police stood by helplessly. At the South End of the city there was a scene of the wildest disorder. Armed hoodlums took over traffic and beat anyone who questioned their authority, even the chief of police, who had to flee the city for his life.

Thousands of outsiders were now pouring into Flint with guns, clubs, and other weapons. Citizens began mobilizing as control of the city slipped into the hands of the crowd. The UAW men in control of Fisher Body plant No. 1 prepared to resist any attempt to oust them. They were armed with 20-inch clubs, guns, truck stakes, wrenches, box lumber, chromium hinges, and spuds, which are hoelike tools for scraping floors.

Within the plant, hose was laid and brass nozzles aimed at points of likely attack. Windows were fortified with steel plates. Mayor Harold Bradshaw declared a state of emergency and appealed to the Governor for help, which was denied.

On January 2, Judge Edward Black had handed down an injunction order against the sitdowners. The CIO had negated the order when Lee Pressman discovered that Black owned shares of General Motors stock worth $219,000. After that time, Roosevelt worked himself sore trying to keep on the fence, Ma Perkins's blood pressure went up and down, Lewis glowered and made statements for the press, and Governor Murphy, who thought of himself seriously as a possible candidate for President, sought to give the appearance of doing something without committing himself to any course of action.

On February 2, Judge Paul V. Gadola, who was not a stockholder of General Motors, issued a new injunction. The plants must be cleared. It was Groundhog Day, and John L. Lewis emerged from his office and saw the shadow of possible defeat.

Walter Reuther was one of those hounding him for action, and in desperation Lewis dictated his famous blood-bath telegram to Governor Murphy.

> Unarmed as we are, the introduction of the militia, sheriffs or police with murderous weapons will mean a bloodbath of unarmed workers. We feel it proper to recall to you the assurances that you have given many times publicly that you would not permit force or violence to be used in ousting us from the plant.
>
> . . . The Police of the City of Flint belong to General Motors. The Sheriff of Genesee County belongs to General Motors. The judges of Genesee County belong to General Motors.
>
> . . . It remains to be seen whether the Governor of the State also belongs to General Motors. Governor, we have decided to stay in the plant. We have no illusions about the sacrifices which this decision will entail. We fully expect that if a violent effort is made to oust us, many of us will be killed, and we take this means of making it known to our wives, to our children, to the people of the State of Michigan and the country, that if this result follows from the attempt to eject us, you are the one who must be held responsible for our deaths!

That telegram was the beginning of the end. Lewis arrived in Flint and took his famous walk with William Knudsen. When they returned, Lewis announced that Knudsen had reached an agreement with the UAW as sole bargaining agent.

Other General Motors officials repudiated the agreement, but clearly the fight had gone out of those opposed to the UAW. It was plain that Governor Murphy had little intention of enforcing the injunction. Roosevelt said privately, "I can't order anybody to shoot a lot of trespassers." In his mind the sitdown strikers were mere trespassers.

Ma Perkins reported Roosevelt's attitude as follows: "Well, the sitdown is illegal, but what law are they breaking? The law of trespass, and that is about the only law that could be invoked. And what do you do when a man trespasses on your property? Sure, you order him off. You get the sheriff to order him off if he tries to pitch a tent in your field without permission. If he comes on your place to steal, why, you have him for theft, of course. But shooting it out and killing a lot of people because they have violated the law of trespass somehow offends me. I just don't see that as the answer. The punishment doesn't fit the crime. There must be another way."

If there was another way, Roosevelt, Ma Perkins, and Governor Murphy never found it.

All this time Flint's city manager, John Barringer, was calling in vain for the State Police to step in and restore order. He could not get the Governor. Other officials refused to act. When the State Police finally did reach Flint, they had strict orders not to do anything. They only watched the rioting from safe vantage points.

Barringer's later testimony outlines the tragedy:

"About half past eight word came to the police department . . . A mob was storming the entrance to the first floor of the Fisher Plant No. 2. The riot squad of the Flint police was ordered immediately to the scene. . . . By the time they arrived a first-class fight had started, and the police immediately endeavored to restore order . . . They were greeted by the mob with missiles of all sorts . . . pieces of steel, iron brickbats, milk bottles, and bottles containing acid . . . Victor Reuther was talking from a loud-speaker wagon and was inciting the men to further violence and to combat the police. . . ."

Congressmen heard testimony to the effect that Victor rode from one point to another in a sound truck which played the "Internationale." Witnesses said that Socialists and Communists served as the cadres and shock troops. Under Walter Reuther was a general staff; under Victor, a system of political commissars and a well-organized regular army, with a horde of semi-organized guerrillas.

Lines of communication were carefully planned and maintained; supplies, both food and ammunition, were sent to threatened points. Assembly lines were set up in some of the seized plants to turn out blackjacks of leather-covered metal.

"Knowing that I could not send any additional reserves," Barringer told Congressmen, "I phoned immediately to State Police headquarters. . . . I finally located Governor Murphy by phone and told him the story. He would authorize no help but told us to meet him later at midnight at the Durant Hotel. When the Governor finally arrived at the hotel and started up the elevator to his rooms, he was followed immediately by Roy and Victor Reuther. . . . The Governor conferred with these men for more than three quarters of an hour before he would talk to the mayor and myself and the other city officials. . . .

"After a three-hour conference . . . he still refused to order the 70 or 75 State Police which were in Flint at the time to help our Flint police department to restore order. . . . I told him that our men . . . were virtually surrounded and outnumbered many times . . . and that if they were not allowed to withdraw by the mob . . . they would have to use solid shot and machine guns. This seemed to have no effect on the Governor."

Actual interference came from the La Follette Committee of the Senate, a committee later denounced by Senator La Follette himself for having Communists on its staff. The committee demanded the names of deputies sworn in to help maintain order.

Barringer said the committee was interested only in getting the names of the deputies. Becoming suspicious, he asked if the names would be given to the Reuthers. The investigators said the UAW would have access to the list. Barringer refused to divulge the names of the deputies. He knew what would happen to them.

The strikers held all the trumps. The 26th Infantry, which had been on duty in Flint, was replaced by the 125th Infantry, mainly boys from the Detroit area, and there was open fraternization between the sitdowners and the guardsmen. General Motors itself asked delay in the enforcement of the injunction. GM officials were afraid the workers couldn't be evicted without a pitched battle, and a pitched battle might turn the plants into rubble.

Time was working in favor of the strikers. While General Motors cut dividends, their competitors made hay. Ford rolled ahead on all six. Nash reported its sales doubled. Studebaker jumped production from 6,000 units a month to 7,700.

The February nights were cold, and the sitdown strikers opened all the windows so equipment at the plants would freeze. General Motors knew that wanton damage already ran into millions. It could not stand a greater loss. In one last move it called for a secret ballot of workers to choose their own bargaining agent. The UAW refused this.

On February 11 General Motors capitulated, and the capitulation started a snowball of compulsory unionism rolling downhill. In the years to come, opposition would be beaten down at all auto plants. The UAW membership, once seventy-eight, would swell to 600,000 by 1941.

And the big winner? Lewis, head of the CIO? No. Martin, head of the UAW? Hardly. He wept. The big winner was Walter Reuther, who was named to head the UAW's new General Motors Department. And in time he would win over beetle-browed Lewis and beetle-brained Martin, too.

Beaten, a Man Still May Win

WHEN he was coming thirty years of age, in 1937, the brawlingest, lustiest year of his life—the first full year of marriage with former schoolteacher May Wolf, in the midst of the riotous sitdown strikes with General Motors and Chrysler, the year he headed into a roughhouse with Ford and spoiled for a showdown fight with Homer Martin—in this year of years Walter Reuther found time to search his sociological soul and wonder if he shouldn't quit the Socialist Party.

He was close to the Communists in those days, so close that many thought of him as a Communist. This isn't strange to anyone who knows Walter Reuther. In the period after his return from Russia he had been so uninhibited in his praise of the Soviet experiment that leading Reds looked upon him as a comrade bearing a Made-in-Russia trademark, and Communist Party leaders, one of them the now contrite Louis Budenz, approached him openly and asked him to join the cause.

At the time Reuther was not averse to taking the step. In his mind Communists, Socialists, unionists, anybody opposed to the capitalists were all comrades fighting a common enemy. His philosophy was that of a sociological mousquetaire, one for all, and all for one. He was open to the proposition until he found that, as a Communist, he would have to submit to party discipline. That he would not brook, and he not only turned down the Communist offer, but he also began to wonder if even the chains of socialism might not be somewhat too restrictive for his freewheeling style.

In time he would decide it was too much of a political strait-jacket and withdraw from the Socialist Party over the objection of Norman Thomas himself. But for the moment he remained in the party; he even ran for councilman in Detroit on the Thomas ticket that year, finishing 15th and out of the money with 126,160 votes. That would be his last public appearance as a Socialist.

He remained friendly with the Communists, who constituted, if not the largest, at least the noisiest and most militant bloc in the labor movement, although Communists today say he remained friends only because it served his purpose during the running fight with Homer Martin.

Martin was a strange fish in the labor movement. A theological student at William Jewel College, he was pastor of the Baptist Church at Leeds, Missouri, until the congregation tossed him out because he went overboard in his sympathy for labor. Eloquent, a maker of quaint slogans, Homer Martin just wasn't designed for the rough-and-tumble school of the Detroit Gashouse Gang.

Martin and Walter Reuther were as different as two men

could be, and there was friction between them from the start. It increased during the sitdown strikes, and it got worse when the sitdowns were over and the exultant strikers came back to the General Motors plants with chips on their shoulders. Many of the strike leaders had become shop stewards and were in a position to tell off the so-and-so foremen. If the foremen didn't like it, the stewards could call quickie strikes, and frequently did. In General Motors there were 170 in the five months from February to June 1937, an average of better than one a day. At Ford, where the simmering had risen to a boil and the lid was about to blow off, there were as many as 259 quickie strikes in a single year.

Homer Martin, backed by John L. Lewis, took a strong stand against the wildcat strikes. He wrote General Motors conceding the right to fire wildcat strikers. This was the rocky crag on which he and Walter Reuther split, for Reuther immediately wrote that it "looks very much as though General Motors does not want an agreement with the UAW" and hinted that, unless General Motors accepted the steward system, the union would make life unbearable by renewing large-scale sitdown strikes.

Martin saw clearly that the world of the UAW, no matter how large it would grow, would never be big enough for Homer Martin and Walter Reuther, so he fired Reuther as a UAW organizer, along with Walter's brother Victor and a number of other organizers in their Stalinist clique. At the same time Martin charged that "an outside organization" was attempting to seize control of the UAW.

Martin meant the Communist Party.

The Reds were already claiming credit for winning the sitdown strikes. William Weinstone, secretary of the Michigan district of the Communist Party, wrote in a pamphlet that they had done it in Flint by putting the strike on a war footing, as William Z. Foster, leader of the 1919 steel strike, had recommended more than fifteen years before.

Weinstone said that workers in Detroit, Cleveland, Toledo, Norwood, Akron, and Flint "operated as a single unit, as an army which responded to every critical situation and to every danger. Toledo and Norwood workers came to Flint in the first days of the strike and greatly strengthened the fighting lines."

The militaristic pattern of the strike, according to Weinstone, was primarily responsible for its success. It was a pattern for victory through violence by regimented thousands. The political atmosphere in Washington and Lansing helped. Weinstone said: "Of first-rate importance among the reasons for victory must be considered the attitude of the Government. By the Government I mean in this case the attitude of the Governor of the State of Michigan and of President Roosevelt."

Frank Murphy, whom Roosevelt had brought back from the Philippines to run for Governor and who ran 250,000 votes behind Roosevelt but nevertheless rode into office on his coattails, quoted Roosevelt as saying, "If Communism breaks out in America, it will be in the Detroit area where it will first manifest itself."

In this instance Murphy proved Roosevelt a very excellent prophet, a prophet who incidentally helped his own prophecy to materialize. U.S. Senator Robert La Follette was another Old Mother Hubbard who helped the Commies into the labor cupboard. CIO organizers were accompanied everywhere by special investigators from Washington, who rode in cars with the banner, "United States Senate car, La Follette Civil Liberties Committee Investigators."

The Communists themselves used not so much prophecy

as cold planning. Communist Party chairman Earl Browder had said:

"We industrial unionists are going to take over the industries some day for three very good reasons:

"1. Because we need them.

"2. Because we want them.

"3. Because we have the power to get them."

The man who was to become chairman of the Communist Party, William Foster, drew up a plan of attack for the CIO, which followed his strategy to the letter.

The blueprint suggested nine steps to support the sit-down strikes:

1. Activity among fraternal organizations, which was carried out in two ways. The Fraternal Orders' Committee was formed under the chairmanship of Bill K. Gebert, Communist organizer in Chicago. Top speakers of the caliber of Philip Murray were sent on speaking tours of fraternal organizations.

2. Wider support for the Communist-inspired Workers' Alliance, which was carried out.

3. Extensive use of prominent speakers from the National Negro Congress. This was necessary to counteract the Black Legion and the race hatred in Detroit, which in the Spring of 1943 would produce the worst fighting between blacks and whites since the St. Louis race riots of 1914.

4. Active use of women relatives of strikers. The Emergency Brigade, women auxiliaries, were very active during the sitdown strikes.

5. Employment of children on picket lines. This was tried during the sitdown strikes.

6. Recruitment of educators, writers, artists in support of sitdown strikes. This has been a standard tactic of the CIO ever since.

7. Appointment of a regular staff of lawyers. Foster no sooner recommended this than onto the Detroit stage strutted Lee Pressman, charter member with Alger Hiss of the Harold R. Ware cell in Washington, and Maurice Sugar, Michigan representative of the Communist International Labor Defense. They proved to be important figures during the sitdown, for they were the ones who discovered that Judge Black was a General Motors stockholder.

8. Strong opposition to deportation of foreign-born workers. There was reason for this. Three CIO organizers in the Detroit area alone were aliens illegally in the U.S. They were John Dolphin, Solomon Fine, and Anthony Probe.

9. Refusal to abide by court orders to end sitdowns, and this part of the Communist line was followed by thousands from the lowliest worker to Governor Murphy himself.

That sitdown strikers followed Foster's recommendations well was apparent. Straight from Moscow came praise for a job well done. The March 27, 1937, edition of the New York *Herald Tribune* carried a cable that the Kremlin was mighty pleased at the efficiency with which the Communist Party had collected funds, and the *Daily Worker* had given day-to-day advice on strike strategy.

When these factors are taken into consideration, it becomes obvious that Homer Martin made the biggest mistake of his life when, in one breath, he fired Walter Reuther and mentioned the Communist Party. Reuther's makeup has always included two ingredients, stubbornness and readiness to seize on an opportunity. Martin not only earned Reuther's implacable hatred, he also stiffened his determination to drive Martin out of the UAW. Now the redhead would

not rest until he had Martin down for the count, and to accomplish this result Reuther, who had been skirting the
underbrush of the Communist Party, plunged into its deep-
est woods.

Circumstances gave him a boost.

There is a well-known Communist tactic which may be
called the invitation to martyrdom. Whenever a Commie
orator clambers onto his Union Square soapbox he hopes
the cops will toss him into the pokey. To accomplish this, he
sometimes screams, "Cossack," or "Fascist tool." If it works
he becomes a hero, with resulting publicity for his cause in
the capitalistic press.

Reuther used this invitation to martyrdom in a dramatic
way on May 26, 1937, and made himself a hero in the eyes
of the UAW when he most needed support.

That May the CIO drive to organize workers in motors
and steel was five months old, and two thirds of one industry and more than half of the other had been organized.
But, at that point, the drives were running out of gas. Block-
ing one drive was the Ford Motor Company and in the path
of the other was Republic Steel. It looked as if they might
hold out indefinitely.

Then, in the space of ninety-six hours, came two incidents that were destined, rightly or wrongly, to win wide
public sympathy on the side of those who had instigated
them. In the case of motors it was the Battle of the Overpass
at Ford's huge River Rouge plant. In the case of steel, it
was a pitched battle in South Chicago, with the police opening fire on rioting strikers, killing ten and wounding ninety.
That was May 30, and a memorial day it was.

The UAW had announced to the newspapers that they
would distribute handbills to Ford workmen on May 26.
Newsmen were on hand at the overpass from the trolley

stop to the No. 4 gate. So were a group of clergymen and investigators of the La Follette committeemen. It couldn't have been better staged if William Z. Foster had written the script and Earl Browder had directed the cast.

Reuther must have known what he was in for, but, jaunty, hatless, fresh as if he had just stepped from a tub, he came out of the old bank building where the UAW had established temporary headquarters. Richard T. Frankensteen, the Ford organizer, and he led sixty UAW workers, forty of them women. Near the plant they spread out to cover all the strategic points.

Reuther and Frankensteen took one group up the steps to the overpass. Smiling, chatting with workers, Reuther and his UAW comrades did not let on if they saw the Ford servicemen approaching from No. 4 gate. Flashlights popped, and the pictures taken were a dramatic lot. The first of the series shows the Ford servicemen coming across the overpass. If Ford had been casting for an Edward G. Robinson or a Marlon Brando movie, he couldn't have collected a more formidable bunch—pugs, discharged cops, manhandlers, bullies. Even Harry Bennett, their boss, once said, "They're a lot of tough bastards but every goddam one of them's a gentleman."

The first picture shows them coming, like the approach of doom. They stalked their quarry glumly. This was to be no courtesy call. One of them yelled, "You're on Ford property. Get the hell off here."

The photo has frozen the action for all time. Reuther heard the call. He cocked his head and looked about. The next picture caught Reuther and Frankensteen, each surrounded by five or six men. The manhandlers had pulled Reuther's and Frankensteen's coats up over their heads. Their arms were locked. They couldn't see who hit them.

And they were hit plenty. The manhandlers gave them a real good working over. It was a professional job. Bennett hired only artists at the trade.

The cameramen shot a couple more pictures and took off. They didn't want a taste of the stuff the Ford servicemen were dishing out.

In an exclusive interview in the Communist *Daily Worker*, Frankensteen said, "They knocked me down again, turned me over on my side and began to kick me in the stomach. When I would protect my side they would kick my head. One of the attackers would say, 'That is enough, let him go.' Then they would pick me up and stand me on my feet, but I was no sooner on my feet than they would knock me down again. This went on about five times.

"Every once in a while someone would grind his heel into me. They pulled my legs apart and kicked me in the groin.

"By this time they had me to the steps. I was bounced on each step. As I went down four or five steps I came to a landing. There were four or five more men who proceeded to administer the blows from that place. This continued until they had me in the cinders by the streetcar tracks.

"It was the worst beating I'd ever taken," he said.

Frankensteen, husky 200-pounder who had played football for the University of Dayton, was a sorry mess. Reuther, his lips puffed and his nose bleeding, landed in the cinders alongside Frankensteen. He had taken the beating better than the ex-football player.

William Merriweather's back was broken. Alvin Stickler's head was cracked and he went to the hospital for two months.

The beating ended Reuther's soul searching, temporarily at least. He tucked away the debate with himself over so-

cialism. One promise he made himself, he would crush Henry
Ford. But, before he could crush Ford, he must crush mod-
erate, middle-of-the-road Homer Martin, and to do that he
must work hand in glove with the Communists of the UAW.
Together with them, he would set the snares for Homer
Martin.

Stacking the Cards for a Misdeal

I T was a school of queer fish that gathered at Milwaukee's Eagles Hall one warm night in August 1937. There were characters of many assorted shapes and sizes and of almost every degree of radical persuasion. Stalinists rubbed elbows with Trotzkyites, and Lovestoneites and Norman Thomas Socialists plotted with Wobbly malcontents who were casting about for a protocol that was revolutionary enough to suit their nihilist temperaments.

Many among the gathering, such as Morris Childs, Bill Gebert and Louis Budenz, stood high in the Communist Party. Jack Stachel was a member of the central committee, though known to be a follower of Jay Lovestone, party secretary ousted in 1929 for sympathizing with Nikolai Bukharin, one of the Bolshevik family who dared to cross Papa Stalin and paid the inevitable penalty.

Also at the meeting, called several days before the UAW convention to stack the cards against Homer Martin, was William Weinstone, author of the pamphlet on the sitdown strike and husband of Gertrude Haessler, the Comrade Haessler who led Whittaker Chambers to a Communist cell near the Rutgers campus in New Brunswick, N.J. Others were Ned Spark, Milwaukee district organizer of the Communists, Roy Hudson of New York, and Jack Johnstone of Chicago, both members of the central committee, as well as ninety UAW delegates to the convention who carried Communist Party cards.

Bareheaded among those who went into the hall was Walter Reuther. His face no longer bore telltale marks of the cruel beating he had taken on the Ford overpass three months before. Boldly, a few days earlier, he had gone back to Gate No. 4 of the River Rouge plant to distribute his handbills. Only, this time, 1,000 burly UAW ruffians had gone with him, and the Dearborn police had stood by, and Bennett's servicemen had stood by, without raising a hand, perhaps because they knew that lifting one finger might have been the signal for a battle such as Michigan hadn't seen since the days of the French voyageurs.

Going into Eagles Hall, Walter Reuther alternately grinned and talked earnestly. He was in high spirits. The Communists might have some idea they were going to take over the UAW. Not Walter Reuther. For him, for Wyndham Mortimer, and for Ed Hall the meeting had but one purpose, to hone a sharp knife for the conservative back of Homer Martin. The UAW stood in dire need of major surgery without anesthesia. Once the diseased part had been excoriated, Reuther would take his chances with the ascendant Communists. He felt sure he could handle them. He was riding a riptide of confidence.

On August 25 there was another big powwow with the Reds. This time a whole carload of Commie bigwigs came out from Chicago for the bull session. Reuther and his associates in what was called the Union Party had Ora Gassaway at the caucus. Gassaway was a representative of the national CIO office who had been sent out to the Milwaukee convention by John L. Lewis and David Dubinsky, president of the International Ladies Garment Workers Union.

Reuther and Company gave Gassaway the full treatment. They made him promises, they flattered him and cajoled him. They made Homer Martin look like the most unappetizing specimen of humanity since the Ugly Duchess. Gassaway took it all in stride and played it cagey. He wasn't ready to cut John L. Lewis's throat behind his back. In 1937 no man, not even President Roosevelt, dreamed of daring to cut John L. Lewis's throat, and Lewis was not yet ready to withdraw his support of Martin.

The best-laid plans of mice and men gang aft agley, and when the Unity Party counted noses after the Gassaway caucus, they found they just didn't have the votes to unseat Homer Martin. To make a dark picture darker, they were not even sure of the ones they had. The Commies themselves, the party-line Commies like William Foster, couldn't swear by the Lovestoneites and the Trotzkyites. They might flop over to Martin's side. They might do it ten minutes before the roll-call vote.

As he left the second caucus Walter Reuther knew the Unity Party couldn't beat Martin, not at this convention, anyway. So the Unity Party boys adopted the usual Commie tactic of disruption. They did their best to turn the convention into a madhouse, and the result was that the Milwaukee 1937 convention was the most hectic in the annals of the UAW. Time without number, discussion descended into argument, and argument degenerated into personal attack, and more than once there was threat of a free-for-all. Martin and Reuther did exchange blows, but after the fight at Gate No. 4, it was a tame affair.

Accounts of the affair vary, and all are partisan. Martin taunted Reuther for permitting wildcat strikes. Reuther taunted Martin as a "pimp of the madames of industry." Martin retaliated by calling Reuther the "murderer of Robert Briggs."

Martin was smarting under the sting of being a joint defendant with Reuther in a lawsuit brought by James Briggs. Briggs, only a few days before the convention, filed an action against Martin, Reuther, Mortimer, and Lloyd Jones for the death of his son, Robert Briggs. Young Briggs had been an unwilling participant in a ten-day sitdown at the Bohn Aluminum and Brass Corporation plant. Reuther denied his men had hounded Briggs for his opposition to the strike. But something frightened Briggs out of his wits, and on the night of April 22 he took poison and died.

"Homer, Goddam it, you're murdering every worker in the UAW. And their wives and children. You're a prostitute, a dirty capitalistic prostitute—"

And then the fists flew, until delegates forced their way between the two and they were drawn apart, panting. Reuther's hair had never flamed redder, and Martin's glasses had been jarred crooked on his nose. Still, as far as Reuther was concerned, it all came to naught. After a few more arguments about "outside political groups"—meaning one group, the Communists—and after a few more names had been called and a few more fists had been shaken, the tumult and the shouting died, the smoke of battle cleared away, and Homer Martin was still president of the UAW. He had managed to squeak through.

Now, if the erstwhile Baptist preacher had acted as a prudent man could have been expected to act, he might have remained president of the UAW for a long time to come. Reuther was a harassed man, fighting a war on many fronts. The war with Martin was occupying much of his time, of course, but Reuther was also fighting a civil war inside his own West Side Local No. 174, and within himself he was debating that persistent issue: should he or should he not withdraw from the Socialist party?

Martin made no attempt to compromise with Reuther. He did not even try to take advantage of the many-sided struggle Reuther was waging. His vindictive nature would not permit him to do these things. Reuther and Company had tried to choke off Homer Martin. They had asked for war to the knife, and war to the knife they would get.

No sooner had the votes at the convention shown Martin a winner than he launched an attack on Reuther's stronghold. He suggested that Local No. 174 be broken up into several locals. It was a pill with a sugar coating. By breaking up into several groups, Martin pointed out, members of the local would increase their representation in the parent organization.

The plan proved to be a boomerang. The UAW in general didn't want Local No. 174 to increase its representation, and Local No. 174 didn't want to be broken up into a number of smaller locals. Not only was the proposal summarily defeated at the convention, but in the local elections of March 1938, Local No. 174 reelected Reuther by an overwhelming four-to-one vote.

Although this was a definite repudiation of Martin, he was a man with nine lives and, temporarily at least, the support he had lost because of Reuther's regained strength was counterbalanced by another flip-flop of the Lovestone-ites into his camp.

This, in time, would work to Reuther's advantage, too. Because they had been involved together in the Battle of the Overpass, a certain camaraderie existed between Reuther and Frankensteen, though Frankensteen was Martin's assistant. Using the bond between them, Reuther chipped away at Frankensteen until, in April 1938, Frankensteen came out openly against Martin, and the latter, in a rage, suspended and later ousted Frankensteen, Mortimer, and George Addes. At the June executive decision at which Martin announced the suspension, Reuther was one of those who stalked out.

The internal war flamed into the open, and while the parties in the struggle for power were airing their dirty linen in the press, Frankensteen happened to admit to *New York Times* Labor Editor Louis Stark that he had talked on occasion with Foster and other Commie leaders. In the public confessional Frankensteen said, "I'll talk to anyone about the union."

Martin was immediately the man on the flying trapeze. Now the truth is out, he said; Frankensteen has long been soft putty in the hands of the Communists, and through him they hope to capture the UAW.

This was a playback of the old Reuther refrain. Walter Reuther knew of the defection of the Lovestoneites. He fed the information to Frankensteen, who charged that it was Martin who was playing footsie with the Communists.

"The conspiracy that actually existed," Frankensteen said, "was a conspiracy between Homer Martin and an irresponsible, disruptive, political adventurer and meddler, Jay Lovestone."

And, as an added fillip, Frankensteen and Reuther produced correspondence between Martin and Lovestone to
prove their point. At this stage of affairs both sides began to
romanticize. Lovestone insisted the letter had been stolen
from him by Russian secret police interested in gathering
information about his tie-in with the deviationist Nikolai
Bukharin. This failed to have the desired effect. While no
one believed such a fantastic story, it helped to establish the
authenticity of the correspondence, and Reuther, who had
been playing along with the Communists for years, was
able to pin his crime on Martin. It was an ironic twist of
fate with a vengeance.

By this time John L. Lewis was completely fed up with
Martin. In August, Frankensteen and Reuther appealed to
the CIO president for help. Thugs had invaded Reuther's
home and beaten him to a fare-thee-well. Reuther cried
out that they were Henry Ford's men. It helped a $100,000
suit he had against Ford for the Battle of the Overpass. But
many suspect that Martin had something to do with the incident. At the time, he was going about with a regular army
of bodyguards.

The persons responsible for Reuther's second beating
may never be known. It is not a matter of opinion, however,
that Martin committed a terrible strategic error in the summer of 1938. On hearing that Frankensteen and friends had
gone to Lewis with their complaints, Martin, without waiting for an inkling of what Lewis would do, bleated to high
heaven that the CIO president had no jurisdiction whatsoever in the matter.

Lewis was not the man to be told what he could and
could not do. When the old leader of the mine workers
was shown a marked copy of *The New York Times* of
July 23, 1938, with Martin's statement, "I will not turn

over the international UAW to John L. Lewis," his graying mane stood up in a manner fit to make a Bantu warrior scream, "Simba!" and take to the tall timber.

John L. wasted no time. He went into action like a Sherman tank. Philip Murray and Sidney Hillman were named receivers to take over the bankrupt UAW, and before Homer Martin could yell, "Foul," the fur was flying. It was the case of the Second Triumvirate all over again, and Martin was the unwanted and about-to-be-proscribed Mark Antony. Murray and Hillman were two hatchetmen, and soon heads were rolling in all directions. The officers whom Martin had expelled were reinstated.

In October, Reuther was busy fighting politics. Governor Murphy was running for reelection, and Reuther felt the UAW should back him to the hilt. His comrades in the Socialist Party felt he should back the party's candidate. Reuther offered to resign, and this action brought Norman Thomas into the picture. Thomas went to close friends of Reuther's and urged them to prevail on him to stay in the party, because a resignation would be interpreted as a hostile act. Reuther had made up his mind, and once he had reached a decision, he could be a stubborn Dutchman. He had definitely decided that belonging to any party, Socialist or Communist, cramped his style. He would stay in the Socialist Party until the fight with Martin had been settled, one way or another. Then it was quits.

While Reuther was busy with left-wing politics, Martin entered into new negotiations with the Ford Motor Co. These negotiations collapsed ignominiously when another one of his lieutenants deserted him. This time it was husky, easy-going, tobacco-chewing, poker-playing R. J. Thomas, an old-line unionist, who, unlike Reuther, had the strange idea that the purpose of the labor union was to get workers higher pay, shorter hours, and better working conditions and not to dabble in politics, economics, and social planning.

When Thomas deserted Martin, he issued a statement declaring that he had been present at meetings in which Martin had been too cozy with a certain Ford official. They were cooking up a plot, he said, to wean the UAW from the CIO. This was the last straw. After one great convulsive effort, like a dying elephant, Martin stamped and fretted, suspending fifteen of the executive board's twenty-four members, including Reuther.

It was his last act. In March 1939 he led his followers into the American Federation of Labor. They held a rump convention in Detroit, while the main body met at Cleveland and elected as president R. J. Thomas, the corpulent goodfellow. Frankensteen was elected vice president and Addes, secretary. Addes became the power center. It was Addes whom Reuther would have to defeat if he aspired to rise to the top of the UAW.

Meanwhile, Martin, scotched but not killed, tried a coup to show his strength in the UAW-AFL. He called a strike in the Flint plant of General Motors. It fizzled.

Reuther determined to show the Kerensky of the UAW how a strike should be engineered. Reuther's greatest influence lay among the tool and die workers, and he called for them to walk out at the height of the summer retooling season amid the talk of war, whose approaching drumbeats could be heard in the Old Country.

The production workers didn't have to strike, and they loved Walter Reuther for that. With the tool and die workers out, they couldn't work if they wanted to do so, and they collected unemployment insurance while at liberty. It was the kind of a strike the UAW liked.

So it was that Walter Reuther pulled a last, long snook at Homer Martin, whose UAW-AFL lived on, but anemically, and it would never get a much-needed transfusion as long as the redhead controlled the labor blood bank.

Separating the
Men from the Boys

Aᴛ his last press conference which claimed nationwide attention, Homer Martin asked, "What does the public think?"

One newsman present sent to his chief a confidential reply: "Where there is an opinion, it is for Martin. He has a better press agent, a pretty fair radio technique, and pearly teeth."

When they bounced him as editor of the *CIO News*, Martin quipped, "The UAW wants an editor who cannot read or write, make a speech, broadcast or walk. What they want is a mummy, a dummy and a flummy."

So he went out of big-time labor with a slogan on his lips.

And Reuther had General Motors sewed up in one big bargaining bag, with Reuther holding the drawstrings.

He had promised to help make 1940 a big production year. Hitler had let loose the dogs of war, and panzer columns were pounding into the Low Countries, across the border into France.

On Reuther's promise to speed production, Knudsen said, "We hope it will be so."

Reuther admitted, "Our struggle is not ended. We must win new improved conditions."

He wasn't entirely happy with the deal he had made. He would never be satisfied with any deal he consummated. As he would explain in years to come, you have to "go back to the bargaining table again and again and again, and ask for more and more and more."

He had other irons in the fire, and for the time being he would shove General Motors onto the back burners to simmer for a time. Right now Ford was the nut to crack. And what a tough nut Ford was. The River Rouge was like an impregnable medieval fortress, with thronging retainers, a drawbridge and a moat, the distant, withdrawn, legendary figure of Henry Ford, and Harry Bennett the ever-ready seneschal watching over his affairs.

Other matters engaged Reuther's attention with more compelling urgency. While doing all he could to whip up the war fever, he desperately pulled strings to keep his own precious hide out of the army. He took a more intimate hand in production matters. Plans to step up American aircraft output fulminated from his brain. He was close to the White House now, close enough so that Franklin and Eleanor Roosevelt now and then would look down from their private political Nirvana and, with a condescending nod, acknowledge the presence of the busy redhead. This was because Reuther was plumping for a Rooseveltian third term, and the President smiled beneficently and bestowed a kingly "Stout fella" on anybody who intended to support him in the forthcoming struggle against tradition, Wendell Willkie, and John L. Lewis.

"Simba" was definitely not a third termite. He stumped for Willkie, not because Willkie's middle name was Lewis but because he was on the outs with the Great White Father, and he often looked askance at Reuther, the young upstart, in the way an old lion turns and looks upon the hyenas that dog his footsteps and will continue to dog them until they know the old fellow's toothless gums no longer can resist their combined attack.

On all these matters we will look in time.

Right now we must concern ourselves with the fall of Ford.

> *Great Caesar fell.*
> *O, what a fall was there, my countrymen!*

It has been the custom of intellectuals for the last generation to sneer at Henry Ford. Sneering at success is not difficult. Big men make big targets, and are not easily missed. Ford, like all men, had open chinks in his armor. These could be enlarged, and little men could peep through and gawk at the naked ugliness within.

Henry Ford was not a complex character. He had the personality and mentality of a country storekeeper, a cracker-barrel philosophy, and a love for tried and true American institutions. Imposed on this rather commonplace foundation was an inventive genius which was to take America off its feet and put it on the seat of a Model T.

In 1937 Ford was 74 years old. He had refused to bargain with the unions in the days of the sitdown strikes, saying, "Labor-union organizers are the worst thing that ever struck the earth," and gave Harry Bennett a free hand to keep up the guard of the Ford plants.

Bennett was as much a product of Henry Ford as the flivver. A former Navy boxer, he came to the Ford plant as a clerk. Something about Bennett impressed Ford, who made him first a watchman, later on the keeper of Ford security. By the time the management-labor struggle came to a head at Ford, Bennett ruled the Ford Service Department, an organization of 3,000 ex-pugs, former cops, gangsters, and men released from prison. It was company goon matching labor goon, but instead of cowing Reuther, Frankensteen, and the others, it made heroes of them.

The years 1937 to 1940 were full of terror, and the terrorists of the union matched the terrorists of Ford. Some of the beaten men actually died. Bennett manhandled men. There was no doubt of that. His plea was that he met fire with fire, that he set a backfire of violence to match the flaming violence of the UAW.

One day he told the press: "I wish to inform you that no labor dispute exists between this company and its employees, despite attempts of certain groups of labor agitators to create the false impression with the public. This is the same group which introduced the sitdown strikes to America and the reign of terror which followed.

"These former sitdowners, whose acts of terror in Michigan industry alone make Jan Valtin's revelations in *Out of the Night* seem like Mother Goose stories, would now sabotage the Defense Program of the nation to satisfy their greed for dues and more dues."

The battlelines were drawn and the UAW heard the challenging cry. It said that Ford once had the highest paid auto workers in the country. Now, the UAW declared, Ford paid only a fraction over ninety cents an hour, while the average for the industry was ninety-five, and Chrysler and General Motors paid over one dollar.

As long as Homer Martin remained president of the UAW, his factional fight with the Unity Party slowed the organizing drive. Whereas, Martin thought Ford was his trump in the internecine wars, Ford actually was a mill-stone around his neck which pulled him down and out of the fight. With Martin out of the way, the drive to organize Ford gathered steam. A large fund, in which the CIO matched the total put up by the UAW, was pledged to the task of cracking Ford. The organizing committee sponsored a special series of foreign-language radio broadcasts. A special drive was aimed at the Negro workers, most of whom were too frightened of Harry Bennett to be scared of the UAW. Every CIO member in the Detroit area, regardless of color or creed, was asked to sign up the "Ford man who lives next door or goes to the same church or is married to your wife's second cousin."

John L. Lewis sent his toughest organizers into the Dearborn area. They were led by Michael Widman. The UAW itself sent a group of able agitators, including Emil Mazey, who would one day be Walter Reuther's righthand man. Mazey was a paradox. He had a smooth, well-groomed exterior and a seemingly gentle manner, but he could put on an industrial glove loaded with lead and lay open a man's cheek with a single, catlike slap.

In 1933, when scarcely twenty, Mazey inspired an Unemployed Citizens League drive to help striking auto workers. By 1935 he had been fired twice for labor agitation—by the Gulf Refining Company and by the Rotary Electric Steel Company. In 1936, working for Briggs, Mazey joined the UAW, was discharged, only to return as head of the

Briggs local and make it the roughest, toughest, fighting-
est local in the whole UAW.

Probably because he was more of the class-conscious radical than the intellectual liberal, Mazey stayed in the Socialist
Party long after Walter Reuther had left. In later years
Mazey would lead the flying squadrons from Briggs into
battle with the Michigan police, stir up GI demobilization
demonstrations while a soldier in the Philippines, and mastermind the long war with the Kohler Company in Wisconsin.

Through November and December 1940 the fire of unrest smoldered in the Ford plant. Walter Reuther was busy
with the other UAW organizers, talking, distributing handbills, organizing. There wasn't as much rough stuff as there
had been. On December 30, 1,000 men struck in the Rouge
River tool-and-die department over rest periods. Ford tried
to discharge the UAW leaders, but the NLRB ordered
twenty-two of them reinstated, and when the union men
heard the news, they marched triumphantly into the plant
flaunting their CIO buttons under the noses of the strong-
arm men of the Service Department. It was something
they wouldn't have dared do a few weeks before.

This was in February 1941, and the UAW, resolved to
bring the matter to a head, filed with the Michigan State
Mediation Board a notice that it intended to strike the
Rouge, Highland Park, and Lincoln plants.

The atmosphere was feverish. The tension was due to
explode.

Dearborn was but the focal point of an uneasiness that
gripped the entire nation. From a labor point of view March
came in like a wild hare and, as it drew to a close, the
President indicated that the country's industrial disorders

might soon compel him to call for more forcible government action. That was, of course, an old refrain from the
White House. Roosevelt had been calling for more forcible government action almost as long as Johnny had been
calling for Philip Morris, and with as little result.

It was an intolerable situation, however, with not only
the Army and the Navy, but half of the world calling for
American arms. More than 400,000 soft-coal miners were
on strike. Although the International Harvester and Beth-
lehem Steel walkouts had been settled, a grim Allis-Chalmers conflict dragged into its tenth week, and the company's
striking workmen were taking apart the Milwaukee plant,
brick by brick. Because of the critical defense orders involved, Wisconsin Governor Julius Heil besought workers
to go back to their jobs. They listened to him respectfully
until he had finished and entered the plant, then they
wrecked his car and fought police until forced back by
tear gas and streams of water from fire hoses.

The strike went on doggedly until Germany attacked
Russia, and then, like so many other Communist-inspired
causes in America, it suddenly changed direction and came
to a halt.

Over this field of conflict Henry Ford towered like a
giant on his pedestal. To America, Ford was the prototype
of eccentric inventive genius. Ford professed to believe in
moderation in all things. But he immoderately hated and
denounced "Jewish Wall Street" and "Jewish Jazz." He
thought "history was bunk." He had sent a Peace Ship to
Europe during World War I and accepted the Grand Cross
of the German Eagle from the Hitler government on the
threshold of World War II.

Despite his eccentricity and his foibles he was beloved
by most of the American people. As late as the fall of

1940, seventy-three per cent of those answering a *Fortune* magazine poll felt he had been "helpful to labor," more helpful than Senator Robert F. Wagner, John L. Lewis, or hand-wringing Ma Perkins.

In many ways Henry Ford was a kindly man. No industrialist hired more crippled and tubercular workmen and former convicts. When he went out on his famous camping trips with Thomas A. Edison and Harvey Firestone, he insisted on being chief-cook-and-bottle-washer so that Edison could sit and give free rein to his inventive genius.

During March the spring freshets of labor unrest came. Shutdown after shutdown racked the Ford empire. Most of them were settled on the union's terms.

Then came April Fool's Day, and both management and labor were in a pixyish mood. To start the day rolling, the company refused to meet with any union committees and followed this up by firing eight committeemen in the rolling-mill, pressed-steel, tire-plant, and B buildings.

When word of the discharges passed through the River Rouge, an amazing and unprecedented thing happened.

"Strike," shouted someone. Another voice took up the cry, "Strike." And soon, louder and bolder, the cries rolled through the plants, "Strike, strike."

It was the strategic minority again.

From plant to plant the word spread and the strike spread.

There had never been anything like it in Ford history.

Men left their lathes and benches. Assembly lines ground to a stop and workers looked about and wondered. Soon they began walking out, first in trickles, soon in columns, and they marched from the Rouge to union hall, half a mile away.

It had been late afternoon when the strike started, and

by nightfall union hall was filled. A memorable night it was to be. All the strike leaders harangued them from the platform. Walter Reuther spoke as he had never spoken before. He recounted their grievances and told them of the great days ahead.

Reuther was only one of many speakers, who included Widman, Thomas, Addes, Richard Leonard, and Emil Mazey, who acted as chairman during the night-long session.

Ford workmen couldn't believe what they had done. It was impossible. Ford was shut down, and the strikers were like kids playing hooky. While Reuther and the others spoke, the workers milled about, talked and laughed, or worried and wondered where the rent was coming from now.

Reuther, Mazey, and Widman were old hands at this sort of thing. They organized soup kitchens, instructed flying squadrons in hit-and-run tactics, set up a hospital because there would be broken heads before peace came to River Rouge again.

To the strikers it was something new and wonderful and frightening. They milled around throughout the dark hours, wondering, worrying their new-found freedom the way a lazing dog worries a bone.

One of the things bothering them was the Rouge. The Ford complex was an island surrounded by huge dikelike walls and a maze of roads. No assault would work here as it had at General Motors and Chrysler in 1937, not without artillery and battering rams to penetrate Harry Bennett's defense lines.

The worriers over the Rouge's impregnability had not counted on Walter Reuther's genius. As usual, the prolific redhead had a plan. It called for a siege, not an attack. Barricades of automobiles were set up at the incoming roads. By dawn the strikers had the Rouge completely invested.

They had not long to wait. Out of Gate No. 4 several hundred Negro workers came charging. Screaming like dervishes, waving six-foot-long swords they had fashioned during the night, they set upon the pickets. Steel pipes and bars described moulinets. Bolts flew like hailstones. Razors and knives flashed in the gray light.

The pickets had not expected so strong a sortie as this, and it was partly successful. The picket line was broken. Some Negro nonunionists fought through to freedom. The rest were beaten back into the plant, not without injury to the pickets. Thirty-four were treated at UAW first-aid stations.

The picket lines were strengthened, and when the second sortie came, about 9 A.M., the pickets met it with baseball bats and hard fists inside gloves reinforced with lead.

The battle was brief and bloody. It was a bum-busting, bushwhacking brawl. A real Pier 6 beef, a Barney. Inside the plant one nonstriker was hanged to a pipe. Outside, one was beaten to death.

The contest was decisive. The UAW once again had demonstrated the practicality of its pattern for conquest through violence. Perhaps the UAW could have been defeated. If so, it would have taken an army to do it, a larger army than the Dearborn police force could have mustered.

After the smoke cleared away, there was a lull. Both sides jockeyed for position. Reuther had long been close to the National Association for the Advancement of Colored People, and on April 5 a group of NAACP officers, including Walter White, pleaded with Negro workers to abandon the Ford plant. Some did. Others left a few days later on the plea of Federal Conciliator James Dewey.

On April 10 the strike came to an abrupt end. Michigan Governor Murray Van Wagoner offered a compromise which both the UAW and Ford accepted. As quickly as it had started, it finished. Henry Ford, for the first time in his life, agreed to negotiate with a labor union.

How the mighty had fallen! It was the end of an era.

Burying the Red Badge

IT is hard to say precisely at what point Walter Reuther found the Marxist approach à *la* Norman Thomas hopelessly academic. In the middle 1930s, immediately after his return from Russia, we see him openly fraternizing with the Communists and Socialists, using them to serve his own ends. His meetings with the Communists in August 1937 were open and notorious. As late as Lincoln's Birthday, 1939, he attended a secret meeting of Communists in Detroit which Browder and Foster called to plan for the future organization of the workers in the automotive industry. This was not long before the final showdown with Ford.

Twenty of the sixty members of the Communist Party's national committee were in on this meeting.

All through this period Walter Reuther was so closely

identified with the Communists that many took him for a party member. According to the Congressional Record, one of those sending greetings to the Second National Negro Congress in Philadelphia, October 15 to 17, 1937, was Walter Reuther, "Communist president of Local 174" of the United Auto Workers.

In the middle 1930s Detroit Communists made a practice of swearing they couldn't pay for medical examinations and treatments and got them on the municipal cuff. One of the doctors who had a large proportion of these welfare cases was a Dr. E. M. Shafarman, who also seems to have been a one-man medical board passing on the physical fitness of volunteers recruited by the Communists for the Loyalist army in Spain.

Walter and Victor Reuther and their wives all took part in this fraud, according to sworn testimony before Congress, and in one case, a police sergeant testified that Walter Reuther and his wife's names appeared on one voucher amounting to $122.

There was testimony that the Reuthers were receiving good incomes from the Auto Workers at the time they swore they were destitute and entitled to be treated as charity cases.

This was about the time Walter Reuther was helping Anna Louise Strong of the Moscow *Daily News* raise funds for the Spanish Loyalists. He was studying at Brookwood Labor College, the center for Socialist and Communist agitators. His UAW Local No. 174 was referred to in Congressional testimony as "an old soldier's home for discharged Communist Party leaders." On May 11, 1938, when the Communist Party had an organizational meeting in Flint, Walter was headlined as a speaker. When he was unable to appear, Roy took his place, told the audience a man was crazy to put on a soldier's uniform, and stood at the Communist salute, his right fist raised, while the band played the "Internationale."

As we know, about this time Walter found it was not politic to be openly radical. He saw such Reds as Lee Pressman, a charter member of the Ware cell and an official with the Agricultural Adjustment Administration, form the early CIO thinking. He saw what their blueprint for America was: the creation of a huge CIO, amalgamation with and a watering down of the AFL, and then absorption of the farmers in a giant Farmer-Labor Party. With the passage of years the plan has undergone revision. The CIO and the AFL, combined under the inspired leadership of such former Communists as Jay Lovestone, now George Meany's chief speechwriter, will settle for consolidation with the farmers and some small businessmen to gain control of the Democratic Party.

Reuther's apologia for his political slant was never better expressed than it was in 1951, when he said: "Because we have fought not only for 'bread and butter' issues, but for those issues dear to all good citizens, the CIO has become a potent moral and spiritual force in the nation and in the world. . . . We gained respect not only for our militant fight for economic advances for workers in mill, shop, and factory. We have won respect, during these twenty years, because we have had a program that is morally right; because people have seen, in our program, a charter for a better world, in which there will be recognition of improved human values and the establishment of standards of economic, social, and moral responsibility in the relationship of man to man."

So Walter Reuther cast off the Marxist wolfskin, but, underneath, his veins still ran red with the Marxist life-blood.

The following fragments of dialogue between Reuther and Harry Coen, assistant personnel director at General Motors, at bargaining sessions a few years later, trace the skein of Reuther's thought with its red thread of socialism. He forever fought the world's fight.

COEN: There is nothing sincere in your approach. There hasn't been yet, so far as requesting a public meeting. It is just another chance for you to get up on the soapbox before more people. You know we are all worn out on this thing. It is no news to your people. And you just get a few more people in here to listen to it.

REUTHER: Harry, if it was—

COEN: Keep quiet, will you? You are all wound up. Relax. I have been away hunting for a week. I am in good shape. I can look at this thing in its true perspective and I know it is all horseshit— Is the UAW fighting the fight of the whole world?

REUTHER: We have been fighting to hold prices and increase purchasing power. We are making our little contribution in that respect.

COEN: Why don't you get down to your size and get down to the type of job you are supposed to be doing as a trade-union leader, and talk about money you would like to have for your people and let the labor statesmanship go to hell for a while—

Again, at a later session.

REUTHER: But don't you think it is constructive for us to relate our wages to prices?

COEN: Nobody else is doing that but you. You are the fellow that wants to get the publicity out of this whole thing. You want to enhance your personal political position. That is what the whole show is about—

And again.

REUTHER: I think when monopolies like the aluminum industry, owned 85 per cent nowadays, and magnesium, when the monopolies jeopardize the safety of the country, they can no longer be trusted in private hands to use them for a profit. That is my private philosophy. It hasn't got a damn thing to do with automobiles or industries operating on a nonmonopolistic basis. And it has nothing to do with the wages in this case.

COEN: It all colors your thinking. . . . Do you believe we have to learn to live 50 per cent better, or do you believe first we have to learn to create that much more wealth? What has that got to do with the dividing up the profits and reducing the salaries of the people in the corporation?

REUTHER: Because unless we get a more realistic distribution of America's wealth, we don't get enough to keep this machine going.

COEN: There it is again. You can't talk about this thing without exposing your socialistic desires.

REUTHER: If fighting for more equal and equitable distribution of the wealth of this country is socialistic, I stand guilty of being a Socialist.

COEN: I think you are convicted.

REUTHER: I plead guilty—

With such red blood flowing in his veins, Reuther was bound, sooner or later, to swim into Eleanor Roosevelt's ken. She had been cocking her eye to the left since entering politics twenty years before, to keep her husband interested and keep his name in the public eye. The first fish Eleanor

caught on her political line, according to the labor writer
Daniel R. Fusfeld, were Rose Schneider and Maude Schwart
of the Women's Trade Union League. She brought them
home with her and they regaled Franklin with the history of
the trade-union movement, stories of sweatshops and occupational disease and the cooperative movement.

Mrs. Roosevelt remained Reuther's best contact with the
White House, and, as we shall see, she stood him in good
stead when he needed support for one of his "plans."
Reuther himself has put it in these words: "I was a needler.
Every time I saw a problem I'd get working on it. I had
contacts in the Cabinet, the Army, the Navy, and the various
war agencies. I'd get an idea and think, 'Now, who the hell
can I get to work with me on this?' When I was having a
hard time putting over an idea, I could always go to Mrs.
Roosevelt or to Ickes, and in that way get in to see the
President."

John L. Lewis's break with the President was a dramatic
one. It had been brewing since the days of the sitdown
strikes when Lewis accused Roosevelt of duplicity. It reached
a head, according to Lewis's account, on the morning of
October 17, a fortnight before the 1940 election.

The President, in bed, greeted Lewis and said, "John,
sit down over here by my side." There was a pause, and
then he asked, "John, I want your support."

Ever blunt, Lewis replied, "You mean, Mr. President,
you want the CIO's support. If you want the CIO's support, what assurances can you give to the CIO?"

Nettled, the President became crisp in his tone, asking,
"What do you mean? Haven't I always been friendly to
the CIO?" When Lewis failed to reply, Roosevelt demanded angrily, "Haven't I always been a friend of labor,
John?"

"Mr. President, if you are a friend of labor," Lewis boomed, "why is the FBI tapping all my phones, both my home and my office, and why do they have instructions to follow me about?"

"That's not true."

"I say it is true."

"That's a damn lie."

The brows leveled. Lewis said, "Nobody can call John Lewis a liar and least of all Franklin Delano Roosevelt."

Lewis took his coat and hat and started walking out.

"Come back, John, I want to talk to you."

Lewis could make an exit with the dramatic flair of a Noel Coward.

Near the door he paused and said, "My phones are tapped, and they are, and everything I said is true, and whatever I said I know because I can prove it by Frank Murphy, who told me so and who knows about it because he has seen your orders to the FBI to do so."

Lewis said, "Goodby," and afterward he declared, "Roosevelt and I are done."

Eight days later Lewis crossed the Rubicon of the ether waves to tell a listening audience estimated as high as 30,000,000 that he could not support Roosevelt because Roosevelt was working for war. Lewis came out for Wendell Willkie, a man "born to the briar and not to the purple."

Telling the CIO that Roosevelt could not be reelected to a third term without the overwhelming support of labor, Lewis said, "If he is . . . reelected . . . I will accept the results as being the equivalent of a vote of no confidence and will retire as President of the Congress of Industrial Organizations, at its convention in November."

Reuther felt that his strongest chances lay with Roosevelt. Besides, he had tangled with Lewis before, late in

1936, when Lewis wanted to give the CIO priority in organizing the steel industry and Reuther had taken the bit in his teeth with the "spontaneous" sitdown strikes in the automobile industry.

He campaigned openly for Roosevelt and helped to open the gates for the floodtide of votes FDR received.

When Lewis said, "Roosevelt and I are done," he was half right. *He* was done. At the November convention of the CIO, he resigned. He had to, because Simba was rapidly losing his teeth, and grinning hyenas like Reuther never would have let him rest.

As for Reuther, he could see more daylight ahead now. Martin was gone. Lewis was waning. And Reuther's brain was working overtime. It was tossing off ideas the way a jolly Fourth of July skyrocket tosses off sparks. One of them would give him nationwide prominence.

The war was coming. Roosevelt would make sure of that, and Reuther was wading into a crusade to get aid to Britain and prepare the United States for war.

But he would have to lay his plans well. It would never do to get drafted himself.

A Pacifist Plans for War

Iᴛ just happens that I grew up with one of our famous flying generals in the delightful New Jersey borough of Mountain Lakes. I don't recall that he was any braver or stronger than the other lads who played baseball in Nefie's Field or swam in Wildwood Lake. In fact, one snowy evening in the long ago, we had a decided difference atop Morris Avenue hill, which ended up in quite a tussle and he didn't show up as any superman.

But he had tradition behind him. His father was an Army officer, and he walked like the son of an Army officer. The only sports he really cared for were those which made an officer and a gentleman—fencing, riding, gymnastics. He went to West Point where he won the Custer sword, went in for flying, and in World War II became a flying general, leading 250- and 500-plane bombing raids on Hit-

ler's Festung Europa. And one day he died in his flaming
B-17, after ordering his crew to jump to safety.

I'll always be proud that I knew Fred Castle.

Sometimes it seems that his whole life was a preparation
for that last fiery moment when he proved he could die well.

I cannot imagine any background that makes a more
obvious contrast with Walter Reuther's. Grandfather Reuther
had left Mannheim so that his sons might avoid service in
the German Army. His boyhood idol had been Eugene Debs
serving a term in Moundsville Penitentiary for opposing
the Draft Act in World War I. As a youth he had debated
military conscription in the back bedroom at Wheeling, and
at Wayne University he had agitated on the campus against
the ROTC.

With such a pacifist background, it was unlikely he
would run to the nearest recruiting station as soon as the
drums began to roll.

Reuther was 33 years old and in excellent physical
condition when Selective Service called upon young men
to register in 1940. He was examined and found physically
fit, but he pleaded deferment for occupational reasons.

It is important to keep in mind, when one reads the
Draft Board report (which is reproduced in the Appendix
of this book), that Reuther was placed in I-A and included
in a quota of 42 men due to be inducted from the Detroit
area, only to escape in a manner that made Houdini look
like a butter-fingered man with five thumbs.

Reuther pleaded that his business was not only labor
agitation but that he was also a member of the National
Committee on Training within the Industry Division of
the National Defense Advisory Council.

Sic! The nights and suppers with the gods of the White
House were paying off, and Reuther was spoken of as a

special assistant to Sidney Hillman, who was one half of the two-headed Office of Production Management, the other being Knudsen, formerly of General Motors.

Hillman stood close to Roosevelt and was to exercise so much influence in the 1944 Democratic National Convention that "Clear it with Sidney" became the theme song. Even labor circles admitted the Red ties that bound him to communism. The American Labor Party's "Brain Trust," published two years before, had described him thus: "Next to John L. Lewis, Sidney Hillman is the most powerful leader in the C.I.O. Next to Corcoran and Cohen, Franklin D. Roosevelt likes Sidney best. Next to Browder, Hillman is closest to Moscow."

Knudsen, for his part, looked upon Reuther as a sort of talented Peck's bad boy. His paternalistic attitude toward the redhead is shown by one story.

They made a contrasting pair in negotiations. One was gray-haired, bulky, ruddy, and the other, pale, medium-built, rufous.

Once, Knudsen glared across the bargaining table and barked, "Young man, I wish you were selling used cars for us."

Reuther's feelings were hurt. "*Used* cars?" he asked. "Yes, *used* cars. Anybody can sell *new* cars."

What had happened? Reuther had a brainstorm. He had whipped up an idea to use the excess capacity of the assembly lines of the automobile factories to roll out 500 planes a day.

It looked great on paper, and Reuther shot it off like a guided missile straight to the White House—in the nick of time, too, because his Draft Board was breathing hot on his neck.

In the end, however, Reuther, who kept insisting that he

wanted to be deferred only on grounds of occupation, was actually deferred on the grounds of dependency, his wife having quit her job with the UAW to make this possible.

Naturally, Reuther never pursued "any further his objection to such a classification." He had been deferred on a basis he had not put forward. Old Jacob Reuther, who had to leave Germany, and Eugene Debs, who had had to go to jail, must have gaped and grinned in the after world too. That young Walter sure was showing people a thing or two.

Years after, during Harry Truman's police action in Korea, Walter Reuther was to fight for draft deferment for all UAW workers. This is a fact not too widely known, but he fought so well that he got all of industry pretty well steamed up, and a big secret meeting of industrial leaders was held in the exclusive Links Club in New York City.

Reuther never did get the deferments, but he did "get" Charles E. Wilson as Director of the Office of Defense Mobilization. This was General Electric Charlie, not General Motors Charlie. He resigned officially because Truman had "by-passed" him "nine ways from Sunday" in handling the steel dispute, but many of those in the know say he could have kept the job if Walter Reuther's boys had gotten their draft deferments.

In the author's *Give 'em Hell Harry,* an informal biography of President Truman, there is a chapter named "Googols and Pengoes," which describes Washington in the winter of 1940-1941. A portion reads:

All that winter of 1940-1941, America, never ready for war until in it up to her hips, really started girding to take on Frau Germania. The National Guard was called up. Dollar-a-year men flocked to Washington until they were a dime-a-dozen. The government recruited civilian workers by the tens of thousands. Army cantonments and munition plants sprang up like mushrooms. Airplane factories expanded overnight and the Navy began to build the task forces that would replace the Pacific fleet later to be sacrificed at Pearl Harbor.

It was a hectic, expansive, Alice-in-Wonderland world in which a tailor drawing $16 a week in 1939, and operating on little more than a needle and a thread in 1940, but with the right contacts, could sew up orders to make shoulder pads for Army officers' uniforms, float a loan at the bank on the strength of them and make himself enough money in two or or three years to buy himself a modest estate in Westchester County, N.Y.

It was a world to which the irrepressible redhead belonged, and not long after the fall of France, and a few weeks before the Battle of Britain, Walter Reuther, never chestier, never redder of hair, burst into Washington with an idea for sale—free.

It was the Reuther plan to win the war, although he didn't dub it such. His title was "500 Planes a Day."

Reading over the sixteen-page pamphlet seventeen years later, one wonders—not at his far-sightedness, not at his knowledge of Detroit's auto plants, but at the fact that he got anybody to listen to his plan at all. The booklet did little but state what everyone knew already, that auto plants had the unused space, men, and materials to be utilized for airplane production.

In fact, Henry Ford, getting old and a little dreamy, in the spring six months before talked about turning out

1,000 planes a day, but that didn't make his plan twice as good as Walter Reuther's.

Reuther's plan made four points:

1. Automobile factories were to continue turning out 4,000,000 cars a year.
2. Idle facilities of the automobile industry were to be converted to turn out 500 fighter planes of a single type daily.
3. Equipment and manpower of the entire industry were to be pooled in a single, coordinated organization.
4. Labor was to gain a voice, jointly with government and management, in the planning and management decisions of the industry.

It might be well to point out here that the key to many of Reuther's plans is codetermination, active worker participation in the management and profits of industry. He would like to see industry set up on a cartel basis.

Now the capitalistic system is not difficult to understand. It works because it is competitive. It is this open competition in the market place that gives Americans the most and the best at the lowest possible price.

As soon as you put government control over industry, you take the competition out of business and slowly strangle it and the system. That, many fear, is the purpose of Reuther, Leon Keyserling, and so many others of their stripe. They want to scramble our economy so that they will have to be called in to unscramble it.

Down through the years, belief has grown among those who dwell ideologically on the Left Bank that the Reuther plan was a definite blueprint of how to get production of 500 planes a day within a period of six months. It

was nothing of the sort. A few figures were given about idle
machines in some plants, such as idle steam and board ham-
mers in the Chevrolet drop-forge plant in Detroit. It definitely was not a survey of idle machines in the automobile
industry that could be used for production of airplanes. It
volunteered no information whatever as to the extent to
which existing idle machines could be meshed together into
a complete production unit for turning out planes.

The plan itself made this clear. It stated:

> We propose that the President of the United States
> appoint an aviation production board of nine members,
> three representing the government, three representing
> management, and three representing labor. We propose
> that this board be given full authority to organize and
> supervise the mass production of airplanes in the auto-
> mobile and automotive-parts industry.
>
> The first task of the board would be to organize a
> staff of production and tooling engineers and assign them
> to make a plant-by-plant survey of the industry to deter-
> mine the capacity of each plant, and the extent to which
> it is being utilized. The next task of the board would be
> to break down a blueprint of the type of plane chosen for
> mass production into its constituent parts and allocate
> the various parts of the engine, wings, and fuselage among
> the different automotive plants in accordance with their
> unused capacity and the kind of work to which that un-
> used capacity is being adapted. . . .

Obviously, the plan was not a plan at all. Reuther
simply looked at the automobile industry, saw that it was
running at less than capacity, and jumped to the conclusion, for which he offered no evidence in support, that by
the appointment of a government-management-labor board,

a blatant Socialist scheme, the automobile industry could continue to produce 4,000,000 cars a year and turn out 500 planes a day.

In a matter of months automobile production had stopped for the duration and the automobile industry never did turn out 500 planes a day. What one type of plane would it have turned out, anyway? Every schoolboy knows that we had dozens of types of fighter planes alone, and these were improved constantly to keep abreast of the lessons learned in combat.

Even *Time* magazine recognized the socialistic implications of the Reuther plan. It commented on the government-management-labor board, "Everybody would be in one great big and perhaps unhappy family, working under a nine-man board (three for Government, three for Labor and three for Management)."

Reuther claimed the basic idea of the plan as his own. With the typewriter keys of the CIO's Press Bureau clicking an accompaniment, he lugged the bare bones of his brain child to Washington, where he so impressed Murray, Hillman and Assistant Secretary of War Robert P. Patterson that they asked for documentation, whereupon Reuther whipped out a report in time to have it decked out in red ribbon and passed on to the President as a Christmas present.

Roosevelt, always the two-faced keeper of the political door, flashed a broad smile in the direction of Hillman, Murray, and Co. but forwarded the document to certain death at the hands of Knudsen, the hard-headed Dutchman of the OPM, and himself gave the proposal a quick and quiet brushoff at his press conference. "It was," he said, "another idea." And the way he said it was damning with faint praise.

On January 1 the Associated Press ushered in the New

Year with the announcement that the OPM had turned down the plan as impractical. That did it. All the pen-pushing Don Quixotes of the down-trodden leaped to the defense of Walter Reuther. Raymond Clapper, Ernest Lindley, Dorothy Thompson, and Walter Lippmann cried to high heaven in their syndicated columns. Jerome Frank, chairman of the Securities and Exchange Commission, convened a Sunday-morning breakfast at the Cosmos Club in Washington to give such big brains as Lauchlin Currie, administrative assistant to the President, an opportunity to listen to Reuther's lament. Harry Dexter White, known as the waterbug of the Treasury because of the way he skittered about, whom F.B.I. chief J. Edgar Hoover later named, along with Currie, as a Russian spy, was so impressed by the Reuther plan that he got Secretary of the Treasury Henry Morgenthau into the act.

"There is only one thing wrong with the plan," Morgenthau said. "It comes from the wrong source."

That wasn't what production men like Knudsen and Charles E. Wilson of General Motors found wrong with the plan. To them it wasn't a plan at all, but an opinion.

"I am running through my mind what there is in the plan that might be useful," Wilson said on one occasion. "The one suggestion that surplus capacity could be used simply means something that everybody knows, and of course the industry has been doing that right along, not just now, but ever since the beginning of the defense program. I wouldn't call it the Reuther plan, but the suggestion is in there."

The General Motors president told Reuther, "If you're interested in production, I'll give you a job with us."

Both Wilson and Knudsen maintained that the pooling of resources and the establishment of a government-management-labor board were Socialist ideas.

"Men are being drafted," Reuther retorted. "When they are being drafted, why shouldn't corporations be drafted?" He said the automobile companies were afraid they wouldn't be reaping their big profits.

On March 1, several weeks after OPM experts had rejected the Reuther plan, Knudsen sat down with Reuther to discuss it.

"Mr. Knudsen and I had previously met on opposite sides of the table," Reuther said with a wry smile. "I thought on this matter of national defense we might sit on the same side. I was mistaken."

Differences developed almost at once. Conceding that auto plants might stamp out the wings and fuselage of a standard fighter plane without too much difficulty, Knudsen insisted that only a small percentage of the industry's existing plants could be adapted for making the parts of an airplane motor.

It looked like an impasse until Reuther suggested, "Suppose we go through an auto plant with you, go over the machines, and see what we can use and what we can't use."

This seemed good—on the surface. On second thought, who knew what could be used and what could not be used? There were no specifications of the standard fighting plane to be adopted in the Reuther plan. How could anyone decide who could build what until they knew the details of the specifications? It was agreed there had to be blueprints. Who was to supply the blueprints? Afterwards, Knudsen said Reuther had agreed to do it. Reuther said Knudsen was to produce them.

During that lazy summer, when the clank of Hitler's armor was receding eastward into the heartland of distant Russia, the Reuther plan was spoken of less and less. The automobile companies were glad to let it die. They were determined to stand firm against any pooling of men and materials, and especially in connection with any hare-brained Socialist scheme remotely resembling a government-management-labor planning board. With characteristic bluntness, Edward F. McGrady said in comment on the plan, "It can probably be done, but who the hell will pay attention to a squirt of a labor leader?"

On December 7 the nation awoke to the fact that the Japanese Imperial Navy had destroyed or damaged most of the Pacific Fleet. For more than thirty years strategists beginning with Homer Lea had warned that war with Japan was coming and that it would open with a surprise attack on the Pacific Fleet wherever it could be found. President Roosevelt, against all precedent and over the protests of many top admirals, had ordered the fleet tied up, two by two, in the bottleneck of Pearl Harbor, where the Japanese would have no difficulty finding it.

For months, Reuther had no one with whom to debate on his plan except Harold Stassen, young upstart Governor of Minnesota, who would debate an Egyptian mummy if he thought it would get him publicity. Now Reuther and the publicity bureau of the UAW could indulge in the luxury of a hundred "I-told-you-so's."

When it was asked why the government had not placed more defense orders, Patterson put the blame on industry. Testifying before the Tolan Committee on December 23, 1941, he said that, every time the government approached the mass-production industries with the placement of contracts, industrial brass said, "We will take on that job providing you give us a new plant."

The UAW was worried about the future. Leon Henderson had ordered a cut in auto production. Union leaders had to sit back and watch 100,000 to 150,000 workers thrown into the streets by January.

As time went on, it developed that Reuther may not have been as far-visioned as some had thought. The auto companies never could have gone on turning out 4,000,000 cars a year and still meet the challenge of the war. To have flooded the world with a standard fighter plane would have been an absurdity. If anything like that had been attempted, the industry would have been unable to make the contribution it did.

When the war was at its height, according to Francis Walton, the auto industry was employing a million men and women and turning out a billion dollars' worth of armaments a month. It produced a third of the machine guns, almost forty per cent of the aircraft engines and parts, and fifty per cent of the Diesel engines. It made war material costing $29 billion. It built 27,000 complete aircraft, twelve billion small-arms ammunition units, twenty million helmets, six million rifles, two and a half million mines, 4,100 gliders, 9,100 pontoon bridges, 76,000 cooking pots for army field kitchens, and 347 air-raid sirens.

One might say this was a pretty good substitute for 4,000,000 cars a year and 500 planes so standardized that they probably would have been shot down by the German and Japanese planes in droves. Yet, Walton says, none of these vast accomplishments represented what military experts held to be the industry's greatest contribution to the war effort.

Detroit's biggest contribution was motorized transport. Americans, British, French, Russians, and all their allies rode to victory in almost two and a half million trucks and hundreds of thousands of armored scout and command cars.

The auto industry put wheels under field kitchens, field-hospital units, liaison headquarters, electric power plants, telephone exchanges, water-filtering units, and pigeon lofts. It turned out cargo trailers, trucks equipped with earth borers for installing bridge piers, poles for communication lines, and land mines. We couldn't have won the war without the Weasel, the Duck, the half-track, and the quarter-ton, four-by-four truck—the jeep.

Since he must have realized its inadequacy, why, then, did Reuther propose his plan? Was it, as Charles E. Wilson of General Motors declared, just to get publicity? Was it to back up his claim for occupational deferment from the draft? Was it an attempt to secure the jobs of the auto workers? Or was it a bald move to incorporate such Socialist schemes as government-management-labor planning and the recruitment of workers' committees to supervise production? The latter scheme had failed even in Russia.

Who knows what his motive was? Was it merely to take one quick step to codetermination? It could have been that. It could have been any one of a number of other reasons. Reuther's mind is that complex, or, some might say, that devious. It takes many fragments of tile to piece together the mosaic of a man's mind.

As the war swirled across the map of the world, Reuther became a trouble shooter for the War Production Board and the War Department. He assumed problems where he wasn't even wanted. When the Normandie burned and heeled over in New York Harbor, Reuther came right out and said the Navy didn't know what it was doing.

As he said, he always went to Mrs. Roosevelt or Ickes for help. This time it was to the brusque Secretary of the Interior. Reuther borrowed some experts from the Department, picked their brains, and came up with his private scheme to right the Normandie. He submitted it at a Cabinet meeting and attributed the ultimate righting of the Normandie to his heckling and kibitzing. The Normandie heeled over again; he offered no explanation for that.

His UAW-approved biography says, "Probably no American outside of government had made a greater contribution to the war effort than Walter P. Reuther."

That could be an exaggeration. Walton's *The Miracle of World War II,* a definitive book on industry's part in the war, doesn't mention him.

Porkchoppers at Work

THE word "porkchopper" is interesting to a student of the labor-union movement in America. Undoubtedly it is most popular among the auto workers, who use it as a bantering epithet for almost any union official. To other union members, pork chops are wages and a porkchopper is an old-fashioned labor leader who concentrates on getting pay boosts for his boys.

The word has an older and more basic meaning, however, one mentioned by H. L. Mencken in his *The American Language*. The I.W.W.'s, the Wobblies—those unreconstructed rebels of the Socialist movement, meant only one thing when they used the word "porkchopper." To the Wobblies, who felt the one objective of labor unions was the destruction of capitalism, a view still entertained by their successors of the Socialist Labor Party, a porkchopper was a union official who used his position to personal advantage.

In this sense the driving Walter Reuther and the personally ambitious George Addes were true porkchoppers. They had been in the labor movement among the auto workers almost from its inception. They were both strong personalities, and it was inevitable that they, like the little bulls in Ferdinand, would run and jump and butt their heads together. Especially the last.

Born in LaCrosse, Wisconsin, and three years younger than Reuther, Addes had followed much the same road. A Greek type, whose standup hair and sharp eyes gave him the appearance of a wirehair terrier, he proved himself a terrier on the picket lines as early as 1933. In the Toledo Chevrolet strike in 1935 he held out after the AFL's Francis Dillon had conceded defeat. At the organization of the UAW at South Bend in May 1936, Addes fought hard to reject the AFL. When Martin was named president, and Mortimer vice president, Addes was elected secretary-treasurer, while Reuther had to be satisfied with a place on the executive board.

Swarthy, young, hard, shrewd, Addes agitated ahead of the boiling sitdown strikes. Always a sympathizer with communism though perhaps never a Communist, he was one of the five UAW officers whom Martin suspended in June 1938. For that favor he repaid Martin by leading the revolt against him and was reelected secretary-treasurer on the Thomas ticket. He became in fact the leader of the faction, while Reuther again was practically left out in the cold.

For years their paths lay parallel, and Addes had always run even with Reuther or a few steps ahead of him; now they were diametrically opposed, and, being diametrically opposed, they must perforce collide again and again and again, until one of them would be bounced out of the running. Each saw the other as an enemy, and swore one another's political death, vowing each to himself that he would not be the one to go down.

There was reason for the repeated collisions. Thomas, little more than a jovial front man for Addes, was a unionist of the old school who believed in simple bread-and-butter demands at the bargaining table. In time of war, when the strike became an unpatriotic thing, the union as a union would have no role to play. Reuther, on the other hand, wishing to accommodate himself to the war effort, nevertheless saw an opportunity for labor to muscle its way into a new area of economic planning, with Walter Reuther in the role of economic planner.

Thus were the battlelines drawn, and not much was needed to start the musket fire.

In 1941 the union was having growing pains. The UAW, like a fat boy, was bursting out at the seams. In two years it had tripled its membership to about half a million. Its bank book showed an increase of 650 per cent to $439,663, and its name, lengthened with the incorporation of airplane and farm-equipment workers, was now officially the United Auto, Aircraft and Agricultural Implement Workers.

John L. Lewis still had designs on them. Grown old and heavy of foot, Simba moved in on their August 1941 convention in Buffalo with the stealth and subtlety of an elephant crashing through the canebrake. Not deigning to go to Buffalo himself, he worked through a henchman named Allan S. Haywood, who pulled strings from a hotel room and did his utmost to add confusion worse confounded to one of the most riotous UAW conventions on record.

Haywood we will meet again in the 1952 CIO election,

when, after Philip Murray's death, he was to oppose Reuther for the presidency.

When the opening gavel sounded, Reuther and Frankensteen were on one side, which was natural for the two mauled Horatii of the Ford Overpass. Frankensteen was not one to work overtime in the loyalty department, as those who had been through the revolution of 1938 knew. At that time, he had turned his coat from Martin to the Unity Party, and Addes and he had come into possession of the correspondence between Martin and Lovestone. This time he switched from Reuther to Addes, and the riband he got for his coat, to quote the English bard, was the office of vice president.

The powderkeg that touched off the 1941 explosion in the UAW convention was the wildcat strike of North American Aviation workers at Inglewood, California, where Communists led the walkout and held up work on $200 million worth of bombers and pursuit planes. Earlier, the CIO had agreed not to strike, and, when the workers did, FDR ordered the seizure of the plant.

At a press conference the President had made his meaning as clear as could be expected of one who spoke always in parables. When a correspondent asked how the Ford Motor Company could qualify for defense work if it ignored NLRB rulings, Roosevelt commented obliquely that he was reminded of the time he was asked whether the General Motors sitdown strike in Flint was illegal.

"Of course it was illegal," said the Great White Father. "But the question should not have been asked at that time. The authorities had a higher objective in mind. The objective then was to get the men out of the plants without bloodshed, and that was done."

Roosevelt left it up to the White House correspondents

to draw a moral, and they drew it. The Ford Motor Company was up to its ears in trouble with the NLRB. But the United States now had a higher objective, which was national defense, and the objective was going to be attained regardless of Ford's labor policy.

Reuther took a strong stand on the North American Aviation wildcat strike. He wanted the strikers drawn and quartered. The Thomas-Addes-Frankensteen faction's watchword was "Harmony." Reuther cried, "Cheap politics." Frankensteen retorted, "Don't crucify the workers."

R. J. Thomas was like a big, bumbling June bug caught between the window and the screen. He bumped heavily from one side to the other, making a lot of noise but accomplishing very little.

Reuther fought hard at the 1941 convention. In the end he lost because he had not as yet found the touchstone of victory, the right issue which his eloquence could fan into the flame of victory. He could never forgive the Communists now. They were heavily behind Addes. They had stood in the way of a job he had wanted these many years, and he would never forgive them.

It was a blustery, roof-raising convention, and Reuther did win a majority of the executive board. He won a final victory over Lewis, too, for the convention pledged its support of Philip Murray as president of the CIO, and that chilled forever any hope Lewis had of regaining control of the organization he had founded.

That was the situation until the Sunday in 1941 that Japanese planes struck at Pearl Harbor, a blow which changed everything, for afterward it was war, stark war, red war, and America needed every instrument of defense it could get.

About a fortnight after Pearl Harbor, Roosevelt gave one

of his fireside chats, which he concluded with the words: "I congratulate you. I thank you. May I now wish you all a Merry Christmas." And then, with an airy-fairy wave of his hand, and a cheery prestidigitatus, he caused his management-labor conference to disappear.

The management-labor conference had been meeting for days, with Moderator William Davis presiding, and it reported three areas of agreement between management and labor:

1. No strikes or lockouts for the duration.
2. Settlement of all disputes through step-by-step conciliation, mediation and arbitration.
3. Creation of a War Labor Board to handle disputes.

Management had sought a fourth point, no further discussion of the closed shop. Labor would no more give them that than cut off its strong right arm. The workers wanted to discuss nothing else but.

Within a week after Pearl Harbor the executive board of the UAW, now controlled by Walter Reuther, had pledged total support of the war effort. This was all very well. It sounded nice in the headlines, when the drums were rolling and the boys were marching off to die for their country.

It overlooked one important fact, however: that the UAW had been born in the crucible of violence. Its lifeblood was lusty compulsion or the threat of compulsion. It had won most of its demands on the firing line by seizing plants, cracking skulls, and overturning cars. Did the executive board expect the union to postpone its demands and surrender its gains in the name of the war effort?

This question and its corollaries were debated in the union from Pearl Harbor to the Japanese surrender.

The leaders were at first in accord. Thomas and Frankensteen, Reuther and Addes agreed that union desires were to be subordinated to the national effort.

"Are you going to tell the President of the United States to go to hell?" Frankensteen asked the men in the shops.

"More and greater national unity. That's what we need. More and greater national unity," declared Nat Ganley, top Red in the Commie wing of the union.

The leaders managed to sell the rank-and-file a program which was labeled Equality of Sacrifice. It called for:

1. An end to all war profits.
2. No luxuries in wartime.
3. No war millionaires.
4. A check of rising costs and inflation.
5. Rationing of all food, clothing, housing, and other necessities.
6. Security allowances for men in the armed forces.
7. Adjustment in wages to meet living costs.
8. A moratorium on debts.
9. Participation by labor in production planning.
10. Far-sighted planning for the postwar recession.
11. Payment of wages over forty hours to be in nonnegotiable war bonds.

But the unionists soon found they were idle dreamers. Their objections began to find voice in men such as John McGill of the Flint Buick local, who said, "We are not convinced that giving up double time is vital to winning the war. Labor is making sacrifices everywhere. We gave up the right to strike. Our brothers and sons are dying in the trenches. Can anyone show any sign that the men who sign checks have made any sacrifice?"

Opportunity was knocking like mad on Walter Reuther's door, but he was too busy working for the Army as a trouble shooter to recognize it. At the August 1942 convention there was open resentment which found no strong leadership, and the union bosses went on like blithe spirits, although most of the rank-and-file thought them strictly for the birds. All during the convention the butter of harmony was an inch thick. Nat Ganley seconded Victor Reuther's resolution for the establishment of a Second Front in Europe. Walter Reuther heaped praise on George Addes, and George Addes tossed orchids at Walter Reuther.

All of a sudden he realized he had found his touchstone. The Communists were calling for a greater war effort to help Mother Russia. Earl Browder cried out, "It is patriotic to demand increased earnings based on increased production" and suggested that incentive pay would "force better profits on unwilling workers," certainly a strange attitude for a militant Marxist.

In the UAW, George Addes was *en rapport* and introduced a proposal for incentive pay, including piecework. Reuther was shrewd enough to sense that this was unthinkable to union men because it involved a self-imposed speedup. When he opposed it, a labor observer wrote in the *Detroit News* of May 9, 1943, "As of today Reuther is the fair-haired boy of the rank-and-file."

He had acted in the nick of time to oppose the freezing of wages and manpower, withdrawing from the War Manpower Commission in protest, and he was firm in his objection to the incentive-pay system in the automobile industry.

In February of that year he had put forward another

one of his plans, this one a forerunner of his guaranteed annual wage. The blueprint called for "full employment" in war plants. Those which couldn't provide forty hours of work a week were to give forty hours of pay, and the cost was to be borne by the government when national shortages were to blame.

He also knew how to turn a publicity trick or two. Early in the spring of 1943 he took 250 shop stewards to Indiana's Camp Atterbury, where they dug trenches, stumbled across swaying bridges, paddled assault boats, and heard the instructor's bark: "Be ruthless—kill, maim, gouge his eyes, stick your fingers up his nostrils, kick him in the balls."

It was great training for the picket lines that would inevitably come after the war. Reuther knew the wage dog was chasing the price tail in ever faster circles. The rank-and-file resented more and more the pledge not to strike. In Grand Rapids, in September 1944, they openly booed R. J. Thomas when he said if the no-strike pledge was rescinded he wouldn't run again.

"That's a promise," Reuther told himself.

"The Union Makes Us Strong"

REUTHER knew that to strike George Addes a fatal blow he would have to set his sights above the picket line and aim higher than peanut politics. These things he could do. He alone of the UAW's porkchoppers was able to consider union demands in their broad sweep and to plan strike strategy in the grand manner.

This time, as always, he laid his foundation well. No one thought it significant when, in the last throes of the war with Japan, on June 30, 1945, he submitted an economic brief to the Office of War Mobilization and Reconversion, the War Labor Board, and the Office of Price Administration.

Why should anyone notice? After all, Reuther was always proposing a plan to someone. Not long before, he had submitted a plan for postwar housing projects. Why should anyone notice one more? Besides, every one he proposed had a socialistic twist.

The central idea of this brief was simplicity itself. "Labor contends that the economic facts of life prove that wages can be increased without increasing prices," he wrote.

"Increased production must be supported by increased consumption, and increased consumption will be possible only through increased wages."

He posed the basic question: "Where will American labor's improved wage status come from?"

Then he posed his answer: "Industry can pay higher wages out of the high profits it is making. It will not have to charge higher prices."

Anyone who thinks about this argument, which Reuther has revived in 1958, can see the fallacy in it. Employment cost, or the cost of labor, constitutes 75 to 85 per cent of the cost of any product. To stay in business, management must translate this increasing cost into higher prices, and when this wage-price increase is repeated, year after year, it reflects itself in inflation. For, to supply money for the higher wages and higher prices, more paper dollars must be printed, and as paper dollars become more plentiful they become lower in value.

The hole in Reuther's economic thinking consists in the assumption that prosperity can be bought or purchasing power given in amounts of paper money. The power to purchase is what the dollar will buy. Plentiful dollars will buy less per dollar than scarce dollars.

The extreme example of false purchasing power came during World War II. One of the officials of the Chinese Nationalist Government was a gentleman named Wu, and a wirephoto showed him after cashing his monthly paycheck. He was taking his pay home in a small truck. The caption under the picture read, "Woe is Wu."

As everyone in America should know by this time, it has

been repeated so often, there is a Chinese proverb which says, "A picture tells more than a thousand words." Certainly, the photograph of Wu told a story of misplaced faith in the purchasing-power theory.

In all ages and climes there has always been a mysterious telepathy between great minds. In Washington it is called lobbying, although it may also take forms that are more occult, albeit of equal potency. By whatever route it went, Reuther's message got to the White House, and two days after the surrender of Japan, President Truman proclaimed executive order 9599, which permitted wage increases on condition they did not result in price increases.

Reuther was hitting on all eight now, and scarcely had another two days gone by when, on August 18, he filed a brief with General Motors demanding a 30 per cent wage increase without any increase in the price of cars.

He also filed briefs with Ford and Chrysler, making it clear at a special executive board meeting of the UAW on September 22, however, that the Ford and Chrysler briefs were only diversionary moves. Although he planned a drive against the automotive industry, the attacks were to be made "one at a time," and General Motors was to be his first target.

Reuther's strategy looked good. The 30 per cent increase looked reasonable to the workers. It would make up the loss in take-home pay resulting from the disappearance of eight hours' overtime when the work week was cut back from forty-eight to forty hours a week. The union had a $4 million war chest to back its demand.

The plan looked good from another viewpoint. He couldn't have picked a better time, because, to make a crude pun, by striking now the auto workers would catch General Motors with their plants down. The corporation had been sweating to reconvert its 102 plants. It had hundreds of miles of new conveyors. First to get back in production was the Oldsmobile Division in August. Only in mid-September had the first Cadillac come glistening from the new assembly lines. It was the first car General Motors had turned out in five and a half years, and thousands more had to be got rolling soon to make up for the $2 billion in defense contracts which had been canceled right after V-J Day.

Richard Frankensteen was cocky about the strike. Frankensteen, whose middle name was Truman, was running for mayor of Detroit. None was cockier than Reuther, however; he said, "We can send thousands of the 325,000 General Motors workers on fishing trips while a few hundred close one plant."

Knowing the automobile companies were naturally and intensely competitive, Reuther used the old, old technique of "divide and conquer." It seemed to him a sure-fire plan.

No sane General Motors official would sit back and watch the competition gobble up postwar markets, and no sane Chrysler or Ford official would fail to take advantage of the golden opportunity if GM should be closed.

On October 19 actual negotiations opened with Reuther staging a grandstand play. He had his publicity director, Frank Winn, invite reporters into the conference room. General Motors officials refused to negotiate while the press was in the room, which got management off on the wrong foot. Newspaper accounts pointed out that newsmen had been "barred from negotiations at company insistence."

Standing outside the room, reporters could hear Reuther in a long, haranguing monologue, while company representatives listened in stony silence. At the end of the session he came out and made the same speech to newsmen.

Boiled down to its bones, Reuther's speech made three points:

1. Auto workers need a 30 per cent rise to make the same money in a 40-hour week they had been making in a 48-hour week.
2. The company can do this without raising prices because of its wartime profits.
3. If the company doesn't keep workers' income at wartime levels, they will not have enough purchasing power to support a high level of production.

The very next day General Motors President Charles E. Wilson held a press conference and made these points in reply:

1. General Motors couldn't grant a 30 per cent pay increase without a drastic rise in prices.
2. If the demand were granted, other workers would demand increases, farmers would want higher prices, and production costs and the general price level would go still higher.
3. The only way to increase take-home pay to wartime standards was to adopt a 45 or 48-hour week during the period of high consumer demand. If such were the case, production, up 20 per cent, would permit the company to pay higher wages without raising prices.

In the bargaining sessions they went over and over this ground.

"We have said to the corporation, and I repeat, that if we can't prove, based upon the facts, or if the corporation can disprove our facts that we can get a 30 per cent wage increase without price increases, we don't want 30 per cent," Walter Reuther said at one session.

"Who are you going to prove it to?" asked General Motors Vice President Harry Anderson.

"Harry, bring out the facts."

Reuther demanded that General Motors bring out its books and show it could not give wage increases without price increases.

Harry Coen, sitting in for GM at that time, didn't think the man "out on the picket lines cared anything about wage theories."

"What does he care about GM books?" Coen asked.

"He doesn't care anything about GM books providing you make a satisfactory adjustment, give him a satisfactory increase."

"That is right," Coen agreed.

And Reuther caught him on the dialectic hook, "But if you say, 'No dice, we can't give you a wage increase,' he says, 'Let's see your books to see why you can't.'"

At one point Anderson accused Reuther of wanting a strike.

"Harry, Goddam it," Reuther replied, "the way you are going about it, you are forcing us to strike."

Anderson leaned across the table and said, "I will tell you why you want to make a strike out of it."

"Tell us."

"Because you got the boys pretty well stirred up that you want a strike. In addition to that, before you had the first meeting with us, you petitioned the National Labor Relations Board for a strike vote, before you were even in the room."

"Harry," said Reuther, "that is the Goddam law you had passed."

"That we had passed?"

"Sure."

The reply was an unprintable word.

In mid-November there was a rumor that Henry Ford II had offered a wage increase of only twenty-three per cent, seven per cent below the UAW demand. Ford denied it. The UAW played coy. In the midst of the negotiations the story came out that Reuther was driving to replace R. J. Thomas as president. Walter Reuther played coy on that one, too. He couldn't deny what was obviously true.

The rumor of a Ford settlement finally became so strong that Henry Ford II had to come out with a public statement. It was one calculated to pin Reuther's ears back.

"We do not believe that this is the time to settle on general wage increases," Ford said. "The wage rates we will be able to pay will, after reconversion is completed and we have reached volume production, depend entirely on these two questions: whether we are able to keep other costs down while obtaining better productivity from our employees."

Ford charged the checkoff system had brought the UAW $7,799,000, "membership and financial security," while "the company has no compensating security."

There were howls of anguish from the UAW. "A union-busting, irresponsible and strife-provoking document" was what they termed it in public. Privately, they railed at "the white-livered, tit-sucking bastards."

When General Motors offered a ten per cent increase tied to a formula to get higher price levels from the OPA, the UAW rejected it flatly. Reuther counteroffered that the dispute be submitted to arbitration, with both sides agreeing to open all books.

This General Motors rejected, declaring it had no intention to "relinquish its rights to manage its business."

On November 20, 200 union representatives met in the Barlum Hotel in Detroit. Along the mezzanine, newsmen lounged on chintz-covered sofas. Bored yet anxious, they stared at a glass transom covered with cardboard, strained their ears whenever voices, strident and angry, rose above the muffled buzz-buzz.

Suddenly there was a burst of applause, the door was flung open and the UAW representatives came marching out, arm in arm, all of them singing their song "Solidarity Forever" to the tune of the "Battle Hymn of the Republic."

> *They have taken untold millions that they*
> *   never toiled to earn,*
> *But without our brain and muscle not a*
> *   single wheel could turn;*
> *We can break their haughty power, gain*
> *   our freedom when we learn*
> *That the union makes us strong.*

The next morning at 11 o'clock the assembly line stopped in the great Cadillac plant on Clark Street in Detroit. The men had turned out thirty-five cars that morning. But at the moment the representatives had voted, they laid down their tools and ran whooping and hollering out of the plant. It was as if school had been let out.

The story was the same at Fleetwood Plant, at Chevrolet Gear and Axle, at the iron foundry in Saginaw, at Fisher Body Plant in Flint, at Delco-Remy in Muncie, Indiana, at Delco Radio in Kokomo, at the warehouses in Los

Angeles and Denver, at eighty plants in more than fifty cities in nineteen states. Walter Reuther had given the word and 175,000 laid down their tools.

In Detroit the redhead, hatless but with turned-up overcoat collar and scarf, mounted a sound truck to give a pep talk to the workers. Not a rosy picture. There would be no strike benefits paid. In time there would be soup kitchens and a doctor for any member who needed one.

"We will travel the road to the bitter end," he shouted. "We will do it because we know we are right and are working for what is right."

A well-wisher clambered into the truck and clapped Reuther on the back, and Reuther turned to him with a quick grin saying, "Just like old times, isn't it?"

Was it? It was not a strike for union recognition. It was not a strike of desperation. It was not a strike against outrageous working conditions or starvation pay. It was a new kind of strike. What made it new was that Walter Reuther based his arguments on the sweeping effect a pay hike would have on the economy of the country. Better pay would step up wages from coast to coast. It would take the nation to higher production and abundance.

General Motors negotiators needled him.

"Why don't you get down to your size and get down to the type of job you are supposed to be doing as a trade union leader and talk about the money you would like to have for your people and let the labor statesmanship go to hell for a while?" asked Harry Coen.

"I understand you think our position makes it more difficult to work out a solution because we are getting into issues here that lie outside the narrow limits of collective bargaining. Instead of talking about wages, what we want, and sticking to that, we are talking about prices and profits," Reuther replied.

"That is very well stated," was Coen's comment. "Nobody else is doing that but you. You are the fellow that wants to get the publicity out of this whole thing. You want to enhance your own personal political position. That is what the whole show is about."

The strike was nothing like the old sitdown strikes. There was no violence to speak of. The company did obtain a few injunctions, but refrained from employing strikebreakers, and the pickets walked their beats for publicity, precautionary, and morale purposes.

Remembering President Roosevelt and Governor Murphy, Reuther had hoped for help from the White House. Truman dispelled that when he gruffly ordered the men back to work. A few days later, the President recanted and appointed a fact-finding board which he had reason to believe would not look upon labor with unfriendly eyes.

Members of the board were North Carolina Supreme Court Judge Walter P. Tracy, Kansas State College President Milton Eisenhower, and War Labor Board Chairman Lloyd K. Garrison.

The strike dragged on into its fifth week. No settlement was in sight.

"If it goes much longer you make it worse," Reuther warned General Motors. "You turned it on. We have some more panzer divisions to roll out. We have not turned on the full steam yet."

"Does that mean the goon squads are to be called out?" asked General Motors Vice President Harry Anderson.

"It has nothing to do with goon squads. It has everything to do with turning on our economic pressure."

"We are going to give you the demands on the contract changes Monday," said Anderson.

Reuther was hot under the collar. He said, "We will be prepared to discuss these demands in about the same schedule you were prepared to discuss our wage demands. About six weeks from now we will be prepared to talk about those things. And then we will give you the union's demands. For every one you give us we will give you a counterdemand. You ain't fooling anybody."

"You ain't fooling us, either."

The redhead was all wound up by this time. He said, "When a bunch of workers asks for their share you thumb your nose at them, tell them to go to hell, refuse to conciliate, refuse to bargain, refuse to negotiate, refuse to arbitrate. That is the way you do it. You are asking for a fight, and, brother, you are going to get it, and if it is the last thing we do, brother, we are going to sweat this one out to the bitter end. The whole American labor movement is behind us. We are backed to the last goddamn inch."

Some might have faith in the President's fact-finding board. Some might have faith in the negotiations that were now going on at Ford and Chrysler as well as General Motors. But what Reuther hoped for was a kind of nuclear fission. The steelworkers were supposed to strike. The electrical workers were supposed to strike. The packers were supposed to strike. There could be a chain reaction and a radioactive fallout of a million and a quarter labor-union men across the country. That's what Reuther meant when he leaned across the bargaining table and told Harry Anderson, "We are backed to the last Goddamn inch."

Picket Lines and Peanut Politics

T HERE is a moment, at the turn of the tide, when the water hesitates, swirls in the grip of contending forces, uncertain which way to go.

In the beginning of the General Motors strike Walter Reuther could do no wrong. The rank-and-file of the Auto Workers took to the strike enthusiastically. A united labor committee was formed. It included four CIO and four AFL presidents. The Steelworkers contributed $100,000 to the UAW war chest. The Amalgamated Clothing Workers and the International Ladies Garment Workers also chipped in.

From the wheatfields of Montana came 300 carloads of wheat. Other farmers' organizations sent food. Mrs. Roosevelt, Ickes, and Morgenthau got together with other do-gooders such as Henry Luce to form a national committee and raise funds for the strikers. Harry Truman's fact-finding committee was getting down to brass tacks.

Harry Truman had always been somewhat of a household god to the United Auto Workers. The up-coming election in the international union would prove to be one of the big factors in the reelection of Truman in 1948, as will be seen. If the UAW election had not gone the way it did, the union would have supported Henry Wallace, giving him the labor support he needed and probably assuring the election of Thomas E. Dewey.

Knowing that labor was strongly backing Wallace, Truman probably wouldn't have wanted to run and might have done a better sales job of convincing Dwight Eisenhower he should have run as a Democrat. The facts of the matter are that Harry S. did run and has never lost his popularity among the auto workers. Give 'em Hell Harry has been enshrined among the lares and penates of the rank-and-filers. In 1957 the union paid Mrs. Marie Earp, widow of one of Wyatt Earp's nephews, $6,000 for the white frame house in Lamar, Missouri, where Truman was born on May 8, 1884, and where his father in commemoration went out and nailed a mule shoe over the door. Earp had lived in the house when he was town marshal of Lamar.

Yes, in the beginning of the General Motors strike Walter Reuther could do no wrong, and he looked ahead to the time when the chain reaction of what he had started would crackle across the land and more than a million union men would "hit the bricks" and walk the picket lines.

Late in December, Truman's fact-finding committee took hold with such effect that General Motors felt the squeeze. It had asked for a definition of its jurisdiction, and the President replied on December 28 that General Motors' "ability to pay" was a legitimate matter for its investigation.

The lawyer representing General Motors was Walter Gordon Merritt, crusty oldtimer who, after the Danbury Hatters strike in 1902, had sued the union under the antitrust laws and won damages of $200,000 against 191 union members. With all his slipperiness in defending Eugene Debs in the Pullman strike, Clarence Darrow had not entirely dispelled in some minds the theory that a strike was a criminal conspiracy.

Before Truman's fact-finding board, the cards were stacked against him, and Merritt knew it. When the President ruled "ability to pay" within the board's jurisdiction, Merritt filed a final brief.

"One big monopoly union," it stated, "dealing with substantially all production in the industry, asserts as its future policy that it wishes to settle all the problems of wages, prices and profits for the entire industry around the bargaining table. . . .

"The union declares that occasion might arise where it might be necessary for it to consider whether the company is 'paying the president too much money'—whether the directors 'who aren't doing anything might be getting too much money'—whether 'the engineers ought to be sweeping up the shop instead of designing their products'— whether 'the managerial personnel has gone to seed. . . .' "

After asserting that "to yield to such a demand would mean the end of free enterprise," Merritt and the rest of General Motors' delegation stalked out of the session.

His brief expressed the position of the corporation in blunt terms. General Motors, he said, "does not plead inability to pay as a reason for rejecting any wage consideration."

General Motors, he went on, was compelled to approach the union's objective "in making prices and ability to pay its prime issue with regard to the radical ideology which the union has expounded in support of its argument. . . ."

In plain language Merritt said this: not only were the cards stacked against General Motors, but Truman, Reuther, and the fact-finding board played only with the red suits.

It was no surprise when President Truman reported, on January 10, the board's findings that General Motors could pay a 19½-cent hourly wage increase without raising the price of its cars.

Yes, everything seemed to be going Reuther's way. Yet it appeared that Lawyer Merritt was not the only one who had no sympathy with the redhead's economics. Not long after the Truman announcement it became fairly obvious that the striking steelworkers and electrical workers were going to settle for well under the 30 per cent increase Reuther had originally demanded. It was no guarded secret that his whole program left a bad taste in Philip Murray's mouth. As far back as December 1 they had wrangled over Reuther's "phony economics" behind closed doors.

A month later, in January, the CIO president, back from Florida, called Reuther into his green-walled Washington office and told the General Motors negotiator the bargaining facts of life. "Soft-pedal the economics," Murray said, and later explained, "At the moment prices were none of my business."

In the hatchery the Reuther plan against General Motors had looked good. It was novel. It was daring and it had looked as if it might work. As the days dragged by and the boys waited and the signs began to droop on the picket lines, the idea took on a different appearance. A long strike loomed.

Addes and Thomas knew Reuther was out to get them at the March convention, so they piled coal on the smoldering blaze. They denounced Reuther for "sacrificing the GM workers in a long, unnecessary strike." They scorned his "one-at-a-time strategy." Thomas, more open than Murray, delighted in mocking Reuther's "fancy economics." The Communists, the noisiest group behind Addes, scourged Reuther with the lash of ridicule.

Circumstances added to his discomfiture almost daily. Some of the less militant unions signed contracts for hourly pay rises of 18½ cents, less even than the President's fact-finding board had recommended. On February 12 the United Electrical Workers, representing 30,000 strikers, signed at the same figure as General Motors itself, and the UAW shouted, "Traitors." A few days later the Steelworkers settled for 18½ cents and the OPA granted a price increase of about $5 a ton to United States Steel Corporation, which General Motors, heavy purchasers of steel, could cite against the decision of Truman's fact-finding board.

The greatest humiliation was to come. Later in the month UAW men at Chrysler signed at the 18½-cent figure and at Ford they signed for 18 cents. The UAW at General Motors, who were to have been the frontrunners that led the flock into a land of milk and honey, were left pounding the bricks. The flock were safely in the fold, not the fold Reuther had promised, but they were working for higher wages and the General Motors men had nothing but flat bellies and Reuther's demand for a penny more an hour.

For once Reuther was angry, and almost inarticulate. "I won't be made a fool of forever," he shouted at reporters and waggled his red head. "The President's offer of 19½ cents was a compromise of our demand and I will be God-damned if I will compromise a compromise. We are not going to take less than that, and this is all horseshit about going back to work."

John L. Lewis lost no time before he rubbed salt in Reuther's wounds. He told a Congressional committee the government could settle the strike in ten days if the manufacturers were given a fair price. Lewis's attitude was "a plague on both your houses." He termed General Motors' position "dishonest," and Reuther's "stupid."

Next day, when General Motors negotiators slapped Reuther in the face with the Lewis statement, the redhead flared back with the statement that Lewis's theory is "we will soak the public a dollar more per ton of coal, and you get fifty cents of it, and the operator fifty cents. We don't think that is the way to increase purchasing power. We want to increase purchasing power by holding down prices and raising wages so that people can buy more things."

With matters in this state, no one gave Reuther much of a chance of being elected president of the UAW. The return to office of the Thomas-Addes ticket seemed assured. At a critical time Frankensteen, the other Horatius at the Bridge, resigned his post, pledged his supporters to back Thomas and declared ominously, "Let Reuther look out for himself."

Every sign pointed to a Thomas-Addes victory. They had a majority on the executive board and they held the two chief offices in the union.

All over, unions were deserting the Reuther standard and coming to terms. When the electrical workers signed their final agreement they staged a loud, drum-banging victory march only a block from UAW headquarters in Detroit.

Labor peace was in the air. Out in Hollywood two of the

bitterest unions became bosom companions. Motion Picture Costumers Local 705, AFL, won charge of fabric falsies, and Makeup Artists and Hair Stylists Local 706, AFL, got charge of installing the rubber ones. Stars like Hedy LaMarr, Paulette Goddard, Katharine Hepburn and Betty Hutton sighed with relief. Now, facing the day's work, they could really put on a brave front.

But outside eighty-odd General Motors plants UAW pickets disconsolately pounded the bricks. With winter a long way to go and a UAW election coming on.

Counting Noses,
from Left to Right

Aᴏᴄᴛᴇʀ dragging on for 113 days through a long winter of discontent, the strike of the UAW at General Motors was settled in the first few days of spring, only hours before the union's annual convention was to open at Atlantic City.

It was a bitter pill for Reuther to swallow. Rationalize it as he would, Reuther had failed to gain his objective. The 18½-cent-an-hour figure at which he signed was far below the 30 per cent he had demanded orginally. It was even below the 19½-cent-an-hour figure recommended by the Truman fact-finding board.

In Detroit, pickets who had walked the line for days after settlement of the Chrysler and Ford disputes tore up their signs and disgustedly flung them to the March winds. The Chevrolet local told 235 men to keep marching until the rank and file ratified the agreement, which they did.

Considering his débâcle at General Motors, no one gave Reuther a ghost of a show in his big test with Thomas. But the soothsayers were premature who counted Reuther out. Even though the top echelons were unanimously opposed to Reuther, the same could not be said of the secondary leaders. Local officials, shop committeemen, and stewards formed the hard core of the faithful who responded to the redhead's undoubted genius for leadership.

At the end of the war Russia won significant political victories, blueprinted at Yalta and Potsdam. As the Red Star rose, the Communist Party's prestige ascended with it, and its members became a sassy lot. When the tide of sentiment for Russia turned, and relations between the Western powers and the Soviet Union began to deteriorate, the influence of the Communist Party waned with it.

The longhairs were invariably long-winded, and by April, 1946, workers in the UAW, as well as ordinary Americans elsewhere, were weary of taking the sass of the loudmouth Commies. They couldn't match them in dialectic, so they commenced to heckle them whenever they started their long harangues.

When a Communist or a Commie sympathizer rose in a UAW union hall to make a long speech, there invariably came the cluck-cluck, cluck-cluck of one or more Reutherite tongues from the sidelines. The Reds had difficulty talking against such a background of sound.

This was only one of the smart tactics Reuther worked out with August Scholle, president of the Michigan CIO Council. The Council had a summer camp at Port Huron, which Scholle made available for scores of speakers. Trained at the camp, they fanned out and made hundreds of talks for Reuther at the union-hall level.

The name of Gus Scholle is an important one, not only in the CIO but in Michigan politics. In fact, a very interesting book, *The CIO and the Democratic Party* by Fay Calkins, advances the thesis that Scholle, with the approval of Walter Reuther, used power politics to take over the Democratic Party in Michigan.

According to the book, Scholle met with a group of discontented Democrats early in 1947 and laid the foundation for the CIO's infiltration of the party. As a result of this maneuver, the CIO elected a governor. At the Democratic spring convention in 1949, *The New York Times* named Gus Scholle, rather than A. Mennen Williams, as the real head of Michigan's Democrats.

Within a few months Mrs. Nellie Riley, former Democratic National Convention delegate, warned, "Socialists are in complete charge of the Democratic Party machinery." Democratic National Committeeman George Fitzgerald said, "I have watched socialism take over the Democratic Party by Communist process."

He went on to declare that he refused to attend the state convention of his own party, "with storm troopers guarding the doors and the chairman presiding with a baseball bat."

Not three years after Scholle's meeting with the disgruntled Democrats, treasuries of CIO unions in Michigan had directly contributed close to a quarter of a million dollars to candidates in the state.

This Port Huron, Michigan, CIO camp was the school at which Gus Scholle, Hilda Smith, and others trained labor agitators, and the speakers, taught by them, went to bat for Walter Reuther, hammering at the simpler union issues until they had instilled them in the minds of literally thousands of UAW members.

Reuther also won a following among those on the right who wanted to throw out the Communist Party. Among these was the Association of Catholic Trade Unionists, the ACTU, which rallied around Reuther as the standard-bearer in the anti-Communist fight. Well might one observer say, "It was a strange collection but it held together." Reuther, who had led Communists in the first attempt to unseat Homer Martin nine years before, now inspired the insurgents against Thomas, who kept his position partly because of Communist support.

While Reuther and his faction worked like dogs to elect him, Thomas and Addes coasted along, confident of easy victory. They had failed to take into account the rapidity with which the Red Star of Russia was declining and the Communist Party was falling apart. Some of the deterioration was due to internal decay. The party's politburo had just kicked out Earl Browder and installed William Z. Foster, and the boys were still a-feudin', a-fightin', 'n' a-fussin' in their Communist Dogpatch.

The Thomas-Addes faction seemed blind also to the fact that Reuther had developed into a leader of national consequence whose picture now appeared on the cover of *Time* magazine, that he had talents for organization and oratory, and a redheaded, clean-cut, clean-shirted freshness which made him especially attractive to the ladies.

Thomas took time out now and then from his bumbling to cast a few wisecracks in Reuther's direction. In between chaws of his favorite Mail Pouch he said once, "If Reuther is elected he will try to lead the UAW into the American Federation of Labor. The auto workers can look forward to the finest dictatorship the union has ever seen."

Reuther dismissed this as "the ranting of a desperate man."

March departed like a lamb and the United Auto Workers roared into Atlantic City like lions. It was April, and the
crocuses were out, and so were the United Mine Workers.
Come the first minute of All Fools' Day, right after the
witching hour of midnight, and the miners needed only the
flick of John L. Lewis's eyebrows to stack their picks and
go off fishing.

On the flag-draped stage of Atlantic City's Convention
Hall, a woman delegate grabbed the microphone in her hot
little hands and screamed shrilly, "I'm for that swell redhead Walter Reuther."

It was Reuther's turn to chomp on his Beechnut gum
and grin. This was the kind of knockdown, dragout convention he enjoyed. For four furious days and nights they
campaigned.

There was often dirty work at the crossroads. The worst
came for Walter Reuther when Philip Murray brushed him
aside on the stage. When Murray hailed pudgy R. J.
Thomas as "this big guy for whom I have a distinct lik-
ing," Reuther was shocked and furious.

Then it was Thomas's turn to chomp on his Mail Pouch
and grin.

Murray lost no time getting out of town. Perhaps it
was good he did, for the fighting had only started. Undis-
mayed, Reutherites buttonholed delegates along the Board-
walk, in restaurants, bars, hotel rooms. Thomasites did the
same.

Now and then they tried to work the same side of
the street. When they did there were collisions. In the
lobby of the Chelsea Hotel, Reutherites and Thomasites
came to blows. A few bloodied noses and bruised lips, and
the flurry was over. At the Ambassador, mixed-up Reuther-

ite forces fell on one another. It was like the incident in the Russo-Japanese war when two Russian regiments attacked one another by mistake.

Three delegates from South Bend bounded from bar to bar, doing a buck-and-wing and chanting, "Reuther, Reuther, rah! rah! rah!" Thomas forces insisted it should have been "raw, raw, raw."

Reuther's sharp dialectic was at its best in the night caucus sessions, and it was there he won many a convert. He knew that that was his strength, and he scarcely slept during the four-day convention.

The delegates gathered for the great decision in a tense and hysterical atmosphere. In the great, smoky, cavernous hall, there were fist fights, near riots, and the constant quack-quack, quack-quack whenever a Thomas-Addes supporter took the floor.

One by one, the delegations went up to the microphones to vote, and when the poll was finished the tally read, 4,444 for Reuther and 4,320 for Thomas. The redhead had won by 124 votes. He was top dog now.

Thomas stumbled from the stage, weeping and mumbling, "Maybe I didn't do a good enough job, but believe me I tried." In one of the wings of the stage, Reuther was already holding a press conference. He wanted a minimum national wage, conversion of airplane plants to factories for prefabricated houses, and recognition of the theory that ability to pay should be a heavy factor in determining wages.

Reuther's victory was a personal triumph only. Thomas was elected vice president, Addes kept his job as secretary-treasurer, and Richard Leonard, the Ford representative, was named second vice president.

The Thomas-Addes forces captured a dominating majority on the executive board. They had President Reuther boxed in, except for Emil Mazey and two or three others on the board.

Reuther put on a brave front when he addressed the delegates. He said confidently, "I want to take my place at the side of Philip Murray and help carry part of the burden which he has had to carry as the president of our great CIO."

But Murray made it plain in private he wasn't trusting Reuther with any part of the burden. His public statements were less obviously barbed. He assured labor, "Reuther's election is not a catastrophe. I would say Walter Reuther has been contained."

Most of the UAW delegates were afraid to trust any leader. They liked Reuther personally; they feared his "dictatorial ambitions," and they made sure he would reign but not rule.

At the last minute, by slick horse-trading, Reuther managed to wangle the post of education director for his brother Victor. Maybe it wasn't a Pyrrhic victory after all. Education could cover a lot of territory.

The Redhead
Repairs His Fences

Reuther won the UAW election in March, 1946, by ruthlessly attacking the Thomas-Addes faction and its pink, scarlet, crimson, and red constituents. No sooner had the vote been taken and tallied than Reuther the victor stood up and said, "I want now to extend my hand to George Addes, and tell him that together we can unite this organization."

Reuther's shock at Murray's rude brush-off was as nothing compared to the shock he gave many of his most faithful supporters. They would rather have seen him stretch out his hand to a skunk loaded for b'ar.

It was probably a fortunate thing for Reuther that Addes and his Communist friends refused the extended hand. If they had accepted it, Reuther would have been married to the longhairs for a long time. As matters developed, their refusal was a declaration of war, and during the next year and a half, to the annual meeting of November, 1947, proceedings in the UAW were like a bad dream.

The new president did his best to act independently of the executive board, and the executive board put over more than one policy which Reuther had not even had the opportunity to see. Factional fights became the rule rather than the exception. Every meeting was an endless wrangle. The Communists talked and talked and the Reutherites clucked and clucked.

Philip Murray did nothing to pour oil on the troubled waters. Relations grew so strained between him and Reuther that at one point in June, 1946, the redhead attacked Murray at a public meeting and blamed him for the lack of success of the General Motors strike.

"The torch we lit during the General Motors strike," he said in a Flanders Field mood, "was not picked up by the steel workers."

At the Michigan CIO convention, some time later, Reuther showed tremendous strength. Murray was impressed. It was an indication of what was to come at the UAW convention, and the CIO president showed a change of heart from that time on.

Always the shrewd customer, Reuther put Murray on the spot by inviting him to a UAW executive board meeting in October. Murray was not the one to bump his head into stone walls forever. It was at this session that he attacked the Communist Party's "complete moral degeneracy." Reuther grinned and snapped his gum to hear Murray attack George Addes's friends. There would be no more trouble from that quarter. He had Philip Murray's scalp hanging from his belt.

Soon after his election, the New York *Herald Tribune* branded Reuther as a "dangerous and disingenuous opportunist." That he was an opportunist, Reuther showed by the way he took advantage of the Allis-Chalmers strike in Wisconsin.

Walter Geist, who had started his business life as an errand boy and had risen *à la* Horatio Alger to become president in thirty-three years, which is par for the course, was having his troubles with the new generation of working men. In the early days of the war the factory was shut down for three months while the Army waited for turbines and gun parts. For four months, from December, 1945, to April, 1946, some 60,000 had been in and out of the seven Allis-Chalmers plants on such issues as employment practices and union security. In April came the strike which was to last 329 days and produce hardships far worse than the General Motors strike.

The walkout, through its leader Harold Christoffel, was influenced by the Communist Party's drift from Browder revisionism to Foster radicalism. Such violence had not been seen since the Ford strike before the war. In violation of a court injunction, Christoffel's Local 240 tried mass picketing, climaxed in four days of bloody fighting in which West Allis police and pickets slugged it out, toe to toe. High-school students from neighboring towns joined in, and at the height of the riot, 5,000 milled about, with the cops fighting the pickets and the whooping, hollering students peppering both sides with rocks, tomatoes, oranges, and paint bombs.

Reuther leaped into the Allis-Chalmers controversy with both feet. He took an old-line unionist named John Brophy to Milwaukee with him. When it appeared he was making some headway with negotiations, the Thomas-Addes crowd charged he was trying to make a secret deal with management.

After that, Allis-Chalmers was a key issue in the UAW civil war. Later on, Reuther would tell the 1947 convention:

"Our failure at Allis-Chalmers was the result of the open interference on the part of the Communist Party in the affairs of the local union involved. This Communist Party interference served to destroy the confidence and loyalty of the workers in the local strike leadership. It gave the vicious management of this company an all too effective weapon to exploit in breaking the strike. Such incidents as the circulation on the picket line of Communist Party petitions on behalf of the party's gubernatorial candidate afforded the company a perfect basis for its propaganda campaign against the union."

The faction fight went hot and heavy until the spring of 1947. Several years before, the UAW had added Farm Equipment Workers to its name, and very often its jurisdiction overlapped that of the Farm Equipment Workers, CIO, as it had when, in 1946, J. I. Case and Allis-Chalmers farm-equipment workers went on strike and Reuther demanded that the government seize the plants.

Thomas, Addes and Company proposed that this union be brought into the UAW and given 500 votes at the coming convention. This sounded like a good way to end the jurisdictional fight until Reuther took note that the Farm Equipment Workers were Communist dominated, that they would probably vote until death for Thomas-Addes and undoubtedly ensure their election in the fall. When he realized that this would be fatal to him, he opposed the absorption with all his vigor; the war was still going on in 1949 when, in Moline, Illinois, a fierce battle broke out in machine shops.

Some of the propaganda became ridiculous. Drew Pearson broadcast a report that Reuther would run for national office with Senator Robert A. Taft. The Thomas-Addes group put out a pamphlet calling Reuther "The Bosses' Boy." When his name was linked with that of Gerald L. K. Smith, Reuther sued a paper called *FDR* for libel.

UAW life became a round of caucuses as the convention approached. Literature pro and con Reuther, pro and con Thomas, pro and con Addes was printed by the ton. There was one indication of how the wind was blowing: a Thomas slate was beaten in his own local. When the boys went back to Atlantic City the balance of the scales had tipped so far that Thomas and Addes did not even contest Reuther's re-election.

One year and a half after he had given Reuther the brush-off, Murray mounted the stage and cooed: "Walter Reuther was elected to the presidency of the Auto Workers in this very convention hall a year ago last March. I was here. I took his good little right hand in mine and I patted his red locks. Walter, I said; Walter, I am going to support you. He said, Phil, I am going to support you. And he did, and I did."

Thomas, Addes, and Leonard were voted out of office. They went off down the road, forlorn and baggy-panted, like the fadeout of a Charlie Chaplin movie, Addes to get a job running a cabaret, Leonard to work for a time in a machine shop, and Thomas to take a minor post in the CIO.

They could have learned from Homer Martin. You can't beat the redhead.

The Best-laid Plans

THE 18½-cent-an-hour wage increase which labor won from management in 1946 became known as the First Round, because this was the first wage rise given after the war. In 1947 Reuther led the Second Round of wage-increase demands, and during the bargaining sessions connected with these he repeated his ability-to-pay arguments and advanced for the first time his theory of the need for a guaranteed annual wage, a provision which would not be written into an auto contract for another eight years.

This 1947 contract with General Motors, which was for two years, included an escalator clause stipulating that hourly wage rates be pegged to the cost-of-living index of the Bureau of Labor Statistics. By September 1948, workers received a three-cent-an-hour boost under this provision.

Because of events beyond his control, as will be seen, Reuther had almost nothing to do with the Third Round of wage hikes, which Emil Mazey, secretary-treasurer of the union, won from the Chrysler Corporation in the spring of 1948. The UAW got a thirteen-cent-an-hour increase.

Reuther announced the Fourth Round in January 1949. It sought a wage increase, a pension program, and a medical-insurance plan. The first objective was Ford, but a strike over a speedup in the Rouge plant delayed negotiations for twenty-four days.

Backed by a seven-to-one vote of the executive committee for a strike if need be, Reuther pressed his negotiations. As he did so, the Steelworkers opened a campaign similar to Reuther's, for pension and health benefits, and a Truman-appointed fact-finding board, headed by Carroll R. Dougherty, recommended as a settlement a ten-cent-an-hour package as management's contribution to pension and health insurance.

This prompted the Ford Company to offer a compromise program granting a ten-cent-an-hour company-financed welfare plan, as opposed to the original Reuther request for a $100-a-month pension for sixty-year-old workers with twenty-five years of service, plus a medical-insurance program amounting to five per cent of payroll.

By October 1949, differences had been settled on the basis of a program calling for a company-financed pension of $100 a month, including social security, for employees of sixty-five with thirty years of service, and proportionate benefits for those with fewer years of service.

Despite his success at the bargaining table, Reuther has made it clear that such haggling is distasteful to him. He feels, and rightly so, that he casts a shadow far beyond the bargaining table. "I wouldn't be interested for five minutes in a pure labor movement," he has said. "You know, the six-cents-an-hour stuff."

According to A. H. Raskin's article in *The New York Times* of March 3, 1949, Reuther believes industry should cooperate in a voluntary program for expanding production, with the government taking over when intervention seems necessary, and you can imagine that Reuther would say, almost from the word go, that the necessity had arisen.

In maintaining what he calls his broad vision, Reuther has lost no opportunity to keep his name before the public, and the way he has found to do it is to dream up one Reuther plan after another. Starting with his 500-planes-a-day plan, in season and out of season, he has managed to come up with a new Reuther plan on the average of one every six months. And, as J. B. Matthews has pointed out, "all of these Reuther plans have one thing in common: they call for greater and greater government control over all the aspects of our economic life."

James A. Wechsler puts it this way in the March 1948 issue of *Harper's* magazine: "Reuther belongs to the school of thought which visualizes an increasingly 'mixed' economy on the pattern of the American future—a society in which there is a far wider degree of public ownership but in which no wholesale liquidation of private industry is contemplated."

Back in 1944, Reuther said:

I think that we must insist that at this time the national government, both the Administration and Congress, announce, as a matter of national policy, that in the postwar period we will permit free, private enterprise that degree of freedom necessary to make its maximum contribution in terms of employment; but if free, private enterprise fails to meet the requirements of our nation, in the terms of the standard of full employment, then the government will not hesitate to take those steps necessary to insure and maintain those levels of full employment for our people.

I think the government should create an overall agency to regulate and begin to work out plans . . . to plan and to coordinate economic factors in our national economy . . . We have not forgotten that free enterprise did not meet the requirements of war, and it will not meet the requirements of peace.

There is no doubt whatsoever about it: Reuther believes in government regulation of almost everything. In connection with his 500-planes-a-day plan, he suggested a board of nine, made up of three representatives of government, three of industry, and three of labor. All other plans are variations of this industry council.

In 1947 he told the annual convention of the UAW-CIO, in a series of stinging remarks relating to the "exploitation of workers by industry":

I say this convention ought to go on record saying to the government, unless the steel industry is willing to get off their fat bottoms and expand steel production, the government has to step in and do it for the people to protect our economic jobs back in those plants. . . .

. . . we should intensify our work to build Co-ops; built with a democratic control over the distribution machinery of this nation so that we can end the robbery and exploitation that takes place both at the consumers' end and the producer end . . . establish a relationship between workers and farmers, where we get their stuff, they get a decent price, and nobody in the middle robs us . . .

Clearly Reuther accused everybody involved in the "distribution machinery of this country" of engaging in systematic "robbery and exploitation."

In the days when the war was drawing to its painful close, Reuther painted grim pictures of postwar depression, mass unemployment, and economic chaos. It was only natural he should concoct a prescription for social health. He dreamed up, and did his best to sell, a Peace Production Board, which would serve as an "economic high command" with full authority to enforce its decisions.

Reuther saw the scope of the PPB as total and totalitarian. Modeled after Benito Mussolini's social dream of the 1920s, it would have full control over materials, allocation of manpower, prices, tooling, facilities, new patents, the migration of farm hands, distribution of goods under "social priorities," manufacturing quotas, and types of goods to be produced.

Overseeing this PPB would be industrial councils composed of labor, management, and government, which would draw up the overall plans. Reuther had learned his lessons in Russia well. It was the conception of a gigantic, all-powerful Politburo for American Business. Leslie Avery, assistant vice president of public relations with the National Association of Manufacturers, wrote a letter to Victor Riesel, newspaper columnist, in which he gave a detailed analysis of Reuther's ambitions. The letter (reproduced in Appendix B of this book) shows how his schemes all parallel German socialistic codetermination.

Reuther, like the German Socialists, is playing for keeps.

Typical of his ambitious plans was one in the late winter

of 1949 designed to use idle aircraft plants to produce low-price prefabricated houses. He suggested that the plan would cost $120,000,000,000 over a period of sixty years.

If all possible mass-production economies were realized, Reuther estimated that a two-bedroom house could be manufactured for $6,000. He got the total $120,000,000,000 by multiplying 20,000,000 houses by his $6,000 estimate.

Fortunately, no one took this plan seriously. Americans living in 20,000,000 boxes, all alike, was a coast-to-coast game of monopoly too horrible to contemplate.

The following years, he had abandoned housing for the nonce and had come forward with a 100-year peace offensive that would cost American taxpayers one and one-third trillion dollars.

This plan, calling for the expenditure by the United States of $13,000,000,000 a year from 1950 until 2050, was submitted to President Truman in the dog days of 1950.

There were nine points to this Reuther scheme:

1. The United States would pledge $13,000,000,000 a year for 100 years. This would not be conditional upon payments by other nations.
2. This would be deposited in a special United Nations fund for economic and social construction.
3. Funds would be made available to peoples of all nations, including Russia and its satellites, on equal terms subject to certain conditions.
4. Upon adoption by Congress the proposal would be submitted to the peoples of the world through the United Nations.
5. The United Nations, upon acceptance of the proposal by a majority of its members, would convene an international conference for the purposes of achieving

total disarmament, establishing universal inspection and other security controls and creating an international police force.

6. The United Nations would convene a People's World Assembly for Peace to discuss the proposal and make recommendations.

7. The United Nations would expand agencies and create others needed to administer the program.

8. An agency would be created by the United Nations to employ scientists to develop and apply atomic energy to peacetime use.

9. The United Nations would expand means of mass communication to familiarize the peoples of all nations with the commitment of the United States and other nations.

Where were the huge sums of money to come from? Simple.

Reuther said, "Only the United States has the material resources for the bold, constructive action needed to banish the fear that holds the world paralyzed on dead center, hypnotized by negative values based on men's fears and hatreds."

The Treasury Department was to find new tax sources as the means to finance the plan. Proposed was a 60 per cent "average" tax rate on corporate profits to provide $7,000,-000,000 in increased taxes and restoration of wartime rates on individual gross incomes of $15,000 or more.

By some magic which the plan did not make apparent the entire tax base was broadened automatically, with corporation taxes increasing perhaps $2,000,000,000 because of increased profits from greater production.

Such a plan helps us to understand the mental processes

by which Isabel Paterson reaches the conclusion in *The God of the Machine* that "the harm done by ordinary criminals, murderers, gangsters, and thieves is negligible in comparison with the agony inflicted by the professional 'do-gooders,' who attempt to set themselves up as gods on earth and who would ruthlessly force their views upon all others —with the abiding assurance that the end justifies the means."

When he lay in the hospital, Reuther, unable to move, and shaken by spasms of severe pain, concentrated his attention on the traction pulling his arm. When the doctor came in to check his condition, Reuther brushed aside his questions and told the doctor what was wrong with the traction apparatus. By the time he was ready to leave the hospital he had developed a Reuther plan for reorganizing the entire institution. The staff of surgeons took a dim view of it.

Reuther believes explicitly in health insurance. "Only a millionaire can afford to be sick in America," he has said.

If he had his way there would be no more millionaires to get sick. This would be effected through a ceiling on income.

The idea of such a ceiling comes straight from the Communist Party. In 1928 the party's national platform listed a number of demands, and Number Four called for a "graduated income tax, starting with incomes above $5,000 and increasing gradually so that all incomes over $25,000 per year are confiscated.

By May 1933, soon after the New Deal had taken over and was shaping the brave, new world of the future, the Reds in the Agricultural Adjustment Administration, led by Lee Pressman, Harry Dexter White, and their ilk, called a Continental Congress of Workers and Farmers for Economic Reconstruction. This "Congress" passed a resolution, among others, "that the Continental Congress demands greatly increased income, inheritance and gift taxation in the United States, and that in addition all income above $25,000 a year be recaptured by the government."

During the depression years few people made $25,000 a year, but the red thread of salary limitations was not forgotten, and in the early boom years of the war the UAW-CIO inserted an advertisement in leading newspapers across the country with this scare headline:

"NO LUXURIES IN WARTIME—NO WAR MILLIONAIRES."

One sentence read:

"By legislation, no individual or family should be permitted to receive in dividends, salaries, or from other sources, income of more than $25,000 per year."

Reuther and Frankensteen put a resolution through the executive board of the UAW, and on April 9, 1942, Eleanor Roosevelt, one of Reuther's two major contacts in the White House, reported in her column "My Day" that:

"The executive board [of the UAW] proposed today a legal unit of $25,000 a year on family and individual incomes for the war's duration, in return for which union workers would accept non-negotiable defense bonds in lieu of all overtime pay for more than forty hours a week.

"I am not going to contend that this suggestion is entirely unselfish, but at least it is a constructive suggestion showing that someone is doing some thinking."

On April 27, not much more than a fortnight later, newspapers announced President Roosevelt was laying before Congress a seven-point economic program for this "people's war" to peg the cost of living "near the present levels." There were lids on prices and wages, and a $25,000 limitation on income.

Tinker to Evers to Chance. President Roosevelt had the ball, and this one went: the Communist Party to Lee Pressman of the AAA and the CIO, to the UAW, to Eleanor, to Frank, to Congress.

Luckily, Congress refused to play ball. On September 30, the Senate rejected the proposal, 68 to 12. Roosevelt tried to get around the body block by executive order, and might have succeeded if Congress had not stood in his way at every turn.

At one time, not long before Roosevelt gave his all at Yalta and then came home to die, there was a report that some New Dealers would like to fix the top income at $10,000. This was thought to have died with the Great White Father, until Reuther tangled with Charles R. Sligh, Jr., now executive vice president of the National Association of Manufacturers, on "The American Forum of the Air," September 16, 1951.

A former amateur boxer and national water ski champion, as well as a successful furniture manufacturer, Sligh showed platform footwork as nimble as Reuther's.

SLIGH: Well, I get right back to my first question, and I would like to have you answer it, because it seems that if anybody has much over $4,000 you don't want them to do it, and you talk continually in your program about proportionate shares. In other words, you take income or goods or whatever it is and you find the average. Then you seem to think that anybody that has more than that average is getting too much. Everybody that has less should have more. Now I think . . .

MODERATOR: May he answer that?

REUTHER: Mr. Sligh, this is not a matter of preference. This is a matter . . .

SLIGH: He still hasn't answered my question, though, as to how low he wants the average income of the American person to be. I'd like to know that.

REUTHER: I believe that we ought to tax the luxury incomes—just a moment—until we get down to the level where it begins to bite them like it bites the average family.

SLIGH: Well, where does it bite? That's what I'm still asking you—to please give me the figures at which you think the average American family should be pegged, because that's evidently what you want.

REUTHER: I think that when there are millions of families in America getting less than $1,000 a year income that $10,000 or $12,000 is a good income in this kind of a period for any family.

SLIGH: You think that about $10,000 then is as high as anybody should have?

REUTHER: I think that before you deny children decent shoes in America, people ought to be cut down to that level. That's what I think.

Reuther's thinking at that period may have been influenced by the fact he was then getting $10,000 himself. Since then his salary has been boosted to $22,000, plus a fat expense account, and he could have changed his mind.

When Hanging
Comes Home to the Hangman

$\mathbb{B}$EFORE the 1947 UAW election Reuther had said if his side came through on top he would drink a pony of whiskey and smoke a cigarette. This was a big concession for the redhead. One night, fourteen years before, the brothers Reuther had arrived hot and hungry at the Hofbrauhaus in Munich, and, on Victor's dare, Walter had downed a liter of beer before dinner.

Walter never cared for drinking after that. When he had to take a drink at cocktail parties, he always chose a Manhattan, ate the cherry and put down the glass at the first opportunity.

But when he had gained undisputed control of the UAW in the election of 1947, he was as good as his word. He downed the liquor and pulled at the weed, choking and gagging all the way. In the category of minor vices he was still the YMCA athlete, clean-shirted, freshly showered, shaved. He had risen in the ranks of labor despite, not because of, a lifelong abstention from liquor and tobacco. His stomach simply wouldn't take them. Not even an operation for the removal of his gall bladder on December 16, 1952, would take away his chronic queasiness.

When Walter Reuther took that drink and smoked that cigarette in 1947, some thought he would now become one of the boys. They had another think coming. Still red of face, coughing now and then into his fist, he gravely announced, "Now there'll be no more all-night card games after executive board meetings."

He also purged the old wheelhorses who had stuck to their union jobs like cornplaster. Knowing that for years the Communist Party had been getting revenue from the rackets inside the automobile plants, he began a systematic ouster of Reds. For a long time there had been an unholy alliance of Commies with Detroit's underworld. This combination of longhairs and musclemen, of Pinkos and Purple Gangsters, had run the loan-shark racket and the policy games in the plants, and Reuther wished to cut that financial pipeline once and for all. He could make better use of the funds in the UAW treasury.

Reuther had not been in office six months of his second term when he called an executive board meeting to order in a Detroit hotel room. It was 2:00 P.M., April 20, 1948, and Reuther, tireless worker as always, kept the session going through the dinner hour. When he saw he could not get home to eat he called his wife May and told her to push the stew onto the back burners.

It was half-past nine, and dark, when he drove his 1941 Chevrolet sedan into the garage behind the neat, six-room, white brick-and-frame dwelling on Appolline Road. May switched on the back porch light, and Reuther walked into the kitchen, taking off his coat as he asked his wife something about their five-year-old daughter Linda.

Reuther climbed up on a high stool at the breakfast bar to eat the stew his wife had kept warm. As he chewed the meat and vegetables he leafed through some papers he had brought from the meeting, keeping up a casual conversation with his wife at the same time.

He had no idea that somebody with a 12-gauge shotgun waited in the darkness outside.

The stew finished, Reuther went to the refrigerator for a bowl of fruit salad. He was turning to go back to the breakfast bar and was partly protected by the open door of the refrigerator when there was a sudden bright flash and a stunning roar. The dish of fruit salad flew into a thousand pieces. Four 12-gauge oo shotgun slugs tore along his right arm and into his chest, spinning him about and hurling him to the floor as if he had been clubbed.

May Reuther stood frozen in deep shock. Her husband lay on his back, conscious but motionless, and bleeding freely. Recovering from her momentary paralysis, Mrs. Reuther got towels, knelt, and tried to stop the flow of blood. Aroused by the crash of the shot, neighbors burst into the kitchen, curious and babbling. A doctor arrived and gave first aid. Reuther talked wildly. "Those dirty rats had to shoot a fellow in the back," he said, and there are many who believe that in this first, instinctive cry he leveled an accusation at the unholy alliance of Communists and crime in many of the automotive plants.

Only a moment before the shot he had been facing the window. To reply to a casual remark by Mrs. Reuther, he had twisted about, and the heavy buckshot that would have gouged out his vitals hit him in the arm and expended their force on bone and sinew.

An ambulance rushed him to Grace Hospital, and police stayed on the scene taking the testimony of witnesses. One woman had seen a man's dark form run across the Reuther backyard. Three boys had watched a man leap into a 1947 or 1948 maroon Ford sedan and speed away into the night.

The learned officers of the law went through their mumbo-jumbo. They dusted woodwork with powder. They measured, they photographed and made notes. In the end they decided the culprit was five feet six and right-handed. Reuther, having regained his presence of mind, said, "It could have been management, a Communist, a Fascist, or a screwball. I can't put them in any order."

The UAW and others offered rewards totaling $126,900.

For weeks Reuther lived in a quiet, antiseptic nightmare, the upper part of his body in a plaster cast, his shattered and torn right arm held in traction by cords and pulleys. One fear haunted him. As a boy he had hurt his toe and it had been amputated. He did not want his arm cut off, not his right arm. The doctors did all they could. Occasionally Reuther got shock treatments to keep the arm from stiffening, but he slept only two hours in twenty-four because the doctors wished to keep anesthesia at a minimum. The pain was almost continuous.

When James Wechsler, a kindred soul, came to see him, Reuther told the liberal editor he had dreamed a dream of a united labor front.

Never at a loss to turn something to his advantage, he told Wechsler, "I really think this thing shocked a lot of guys into realizing that unionism is more than a matter of nickels and dimes, and that personal interests and prejudices aren't as important as they seem."

The year 1948 was a big election year, of course, and while he lay in bed the redhead worried about the progress of our economy and the processes of our democracy. That capitalism was sliding down a greased ramp he was convinced. He predicted that a frightful bust was in the offing. There would be 14,000,000 unemployed by 1952.

As for the processes of democracy, he told Wechsler he was afraid "a lot of decent guys" would vote for Henry Wallace if the Democrats renominated Harry Truman. He said he thought it was tragic that Truman had inherited the presidency "at a time when the world needs great leadership." The man to sit in the White House, in his opinion, was that great mountain climber, Supreme Court Justice William O. Douglas. President Roosevelt had wanted Douglas in 1945, too, but Douglas could never quite make the grade.

In Grace Hospital, through the summer, Reuther made his slow recovery, and gradually the citizenry forgot about his attempted murder. And then, one day, police investigating a $600 store burglary in Pontiac, Michigan, picked up the trail of a gent named Carl Bolton.

Bolton had been vice president of UAW Local 400 at the Highland Park plant of the Ford Motor Company. But his term was a short one. He had not been reelected in 1946. For a longer period he had been the mastermind of a gang of petty thieves. The authorities ran him to earth in Indiana and arrested four members of his gang with him.

One, an ex-con named Jack Miller, "spilled his guts." Another, John Pentello, filled in the holes in Miller's story. It looked like the real thing. A few weeks before the Reu-

ther shooting, Bolton, according to stool pigeon Miller, offered him and a pal $15,000 to "bump the Big Guy." Mil-
ler said nix, and, two days before the shooting, Bolton came
to Miller's house and borrowed two shotguns. As he went
off with the tools of his trade, Bolton said, "I got to have
the typewriters. I got to get rid of a Communist son of a
bitch."

Bolton looked as if he were it until May 22, 1949, just
a few minutes before the witching hour of midnight, when a
gunman poked the flat nose of a 12-gauge shotgun through
a window screen and blazed away at Victor Reuther sitting
in his living room. This time there were two explosions,
and Walter's younger brother tumbled forward, like a para-
trooper hitting the silk, his chest and face spouting blood.

He managed to gasp three words, "Call an ambulance."

His wife Sophie ran into the street, screaming, "My
God, Vic's been shot."

Neighbors poked their heads out in time to see a man
sprint across the lawn and a maroon sedan speed away.

Vic, like his older brother, escaped death. But doctors
at Henry Ford Hospital had to remove his right eye.

A little more than a month before, the CIO had bought
Walter an $11,600 Packard armored sedan. Getting out of it,
he looked down at his right arm, still in a sling, and said to
newsmen, "It's not possible. Not both of us. Not twice."

The shotgun, either the same gun or identical with the
one used a year before, was found in a clump of bushes beside the house. It had been wiped clean of fingerprints. A
footprint and the impression of a knee in the ground were
blurred and proved of little value to police.

Inspector Joseph Krug was baffled. He said, "The shooting could have been done by Bolton's friends to take the

heat off Bolton. It could have been done by other groups. It could have been done by a crackpot."

Walter was as vague as he had been since a short time after his own shooting. He said, "The same people who paid to have me shot paid to have my brother shot, and for the same reason."

The Communists were the most likely suspects. More than any group they had reason to hate the Reuthers. The Reds wanted the UAW to stop raiding the Communist-dominated United Electrical Workers Union. They wanted to keep the UAW from absorbing the Farm Equipment Workers Union, except on their own terms. It was a fight that would lead to the ouster of the two unions from the CIO.

The Commies were allied with the numbers racketeers, the bookmakers, and the loan sharks who infested the auto plants. Reuther hated gambling, which he associated with drinking, smoking, and airless rooms, all the things his stomach couldn't take.

The unions and the racketeers have always been closely allied. A whole book could be written on the marriage of gangsterism and trade unionism in New York City alone. The German Mob under Dutch Schultz handled the bakers; the Irish Mob under Owney Madden controlled transportation, building construction, and longshore trade. The Italian Mob under Charles "Lucky" Luciano ruled the fruit and vegetable markets. The Jewish Mob, first under Arnold Rothstein, and later under Louis "Lepke" Buchalter and Jacob "Gurrah" Shapiro, "protected" now management and now the unions in the garment district.

Across the country, in Akron and Cleveland, in Detroit and Chicago, in Kansas City and Hollywood, the same pattern was masterminded by Willie Bioff, Al Capone, George Scalise, Umbrella Mike Boyle, and Max Pollock. Fires were set, elevator cables slipped, acid and stink bombs thrown, trucks overturned and other industrial tortures devised. During the World's Fair of 1933 Pollock organized the pimps and prostitutes and all the queers and freaks in Cash and Carry Pyle's sideshow. Pollock even set fire to the chorus girls' panties in a Chicago tavern to force them into the Retail Grocery Clerks Union, and that shows the ends to which union leaders of that stripe will go, no pun intended.

It's understandable why James R. Hoffa, the new Teamster president, has been quoted as saying, "Trade unionism without strike violence is like a cop without a nightstick."

In Detroit, gambling was big business. It had never been a simon-pure town. The criminal high jinks of such mobs as the Purple Gang won a spot alongside the big syndicates of New York and Chicago. In the decade from 1934 to 1944 the Detroit gangs which Prohibition had spawned worked their way into other lucrative enterprises, legitimate and illegitimate. Gamblers were doing a $75,000,000 annual business in Detroit alone, and almost one third of this was transacted openly in the auto plants themselves. Several big gambling syndicates handled this business, and one of the biggest, operating in several of the Ford plants, was run by a strange assortment of Commie gangsters, white and Negro. One out of every 250 auto workers was keeping book for one of the syndicates, and the racing handbooks took $12,000,000 a year from the pay envelopes of the auto workers, the numbers game took $7,000,000, and baseball pools, $6,000,000. And when they got behind with their rent, the loan sharks clipped the auto workers for plenty.

Never had the legislative mills of Detroit, Lansing, and Washington spun more fustian than they did after the shooting of the second Reuther brother. Never had lawmakers viewed with alarm as they did in the next seventy-two hours.

President George Edwards of the Detroit City Council wrote Senator Hubert M. Humphrey, Minnesota Democrat:

> I am sure you are as concerned as I am about the Victor Reuther shooting. . . . The Mayor and Council of the City of Detroit have officially urged the FBI to co-operate in this case.
>
> I feel we can afford to leave no stone unturned in our attempts to track down the would-be assassins of these two magnificently prodemocratic American labor leaders.
>
> You'll recall that Victor Reuther recently returned from an official mission as representative of the United States government in the ECA program from Europe, where, as chairman of the labor subcommittee, he met with prodemocratic European trade unionists to aid in a fight for European democracy.

Senator Humphrey passed the ball to Attorney General Tom Clark, saying, "I was shocked to learn of the criminal attack upon the life of Victor Reuther."

Bible-toting, Scripture-quoting Senator Charles W. Tobey, New Hampshire Republican, shook his gray poll and called it "a dastardly attempt" on the "life of one of the nation's outstanding labor leaders."

He said, "Organized labor has no more devoted exponent than Walter Reuther. Today I offer my tribute to the man. . . . Express the wish God will spare his life."

Representative Thomas H. Burke of Ohio noted the fact that Victor Reuther was one of the four labor members of the Anglo-American Council on Productivity named by Paul Hoffman, ECA Administrator. Governor Mennen Williams, Senator Homer Ferguson, and Representatives Louis C. Rabaut of Michigan and Charles H. Kersten of Wisconsin spoke long and feelingly on the subject.

"Those who would commit crimes of that kind must be taught the lesson that in America such things cannot be allowed to happen. . . . Too much is enough," said Mr. Rabaut.

Two weeks after Senator Ferguson *et alii* had spoken in Congress, Representative Clare Hoffman, archenemy of Walter Reuther, rose in the House and told his colleagues that the police of Beaumont, Texas, had escorted Herman Brown and his carpenters out of town. Their crime, Hoffman said, was that they had refused to join a union, and Beaumont police refused to protect them. There was no comment from Hoffman's colleagues.

As 1949 waned, a reporter for the *Detroit Times* got an anonymous phone tip that UAW headquarters at Milwaukee and Cass Streets was to be blown up, and a search of the premises by the bomb squad turned up thirty-nine sticks of dynamite taped into three bundles. If the fuses had not been defective, this might have been the obituary, not the biography, of Walter Reuther.

UAW officials were dissatisfied with the way authorities were handling the case. So bitter were they about the fumbling fingers of the long arm of the law that they helped throw out James M. McNally as Wayne County Prosecutor in 1949. His successor, Gerald K. O'Brien, had the embarrassing problem of Bolton on his hands.

Bolton went on trial in January 1950. The trial lasted

a full three weeks, and the star witnesses were Miller and Pentello, who told their stories, which the jury evidently refused to believe.

"Not guilty," said the foreman.

Now, dissatisfied UAW officials hired their own private eyes. They also welcomed with open arms two operatives, Harvey Kennedy and Sam Henderson, who said they had a hot tip that "a hired professional gunman in town knew plenty about the shooting." The private detectives set out on the trail of this suspect, and the police set out on the trail of Kennedy and Henderson. When the cops found that the two private eyes had hired a maroon Ford sedan five hours before the Walter Reuther shooting, they hustled the detecting pair off to the hoosegow and put them on the grill. Then the authorities admitted they were in error and released the two detectives. Kennedy lost no time getting out of town. But Henderson stayed behind, sued for $50,-000, then dropped his suit and continued working for the union.

The investigation developed many interesting angles. In the seven days before he was shot, Walter Reuther had received three threatening letters. One called him an anti-Communist. One accused him of being a pro-Communist. The third damned him for urging auto workers to bowl only on alleys which permitted use by all races and creeds.

His secretary said Reuther was forever being blamed for his aggressive stand against poker and drinking sessions, and for his critical attitude toward betting on the ponies, baseball pools, and policy play during working hours. Police arrested many former officials of Local 600 at Ford, but held only Nelson Davis, a Negro Communist, for any length of time. When Davis was arrested, Inspector Krug warned, "If his identity leaks out, we may have another killing on our hands." A smart mouthpiece got a magistrate to release Davis, who sank back into the Detroit underworld from which he had briefly emerged.

One of the stories Henderson dug up was that two Detroit hoodlums, Sam Scroy and Peter Lucido, had been ready to talk about the Reuther shooting when they suddenly vanished one night, not too many weeks after the shooting. Dame Rumor whispered among the gin mills and bistros that Sam and Peter, who were cousins, had been thoughtfully fitted out with concrete overcoats against the chill air at the bottom of a limestone quarry or the damp ooze of a swamp between Detroit and Toledo.

One person who believed this obituary notice was Chris Scroy, a brother of Sam. He went out gunning for a police character named Sam Stern, but when he had flushed him from cover, his hand had the shakes and he succeeded only in winging him.

A more promising development came when a UAW official, whose identity has been suspected but never proved, was defeated for reelection. One of the detectives hired by the UAW, probably Henderson, found on the desk pad of this defeated UAW official the name of Santo (Sam) Perrone, a squat, balding, wealthy scrapiron dealer and former rumrunner, who had a police record going back to the earliest days of Prohibition. Perrone was known as a union buster among other even more unsavory accomplishments.

When the Senate Crime Investigating Committee came to Detroit in 1951, with its traveling circus and clowns, Perrone and his son-in-law Carl Renda were put on the pan. In 1953 Perrone was fined and put on probation for terrorizing employees who wanted to organize a union in a Detroit firm.

There were other shadows in Perrone's past. In 1945

a woman named Mrs. Lydia Thompson was murdered near Detroit. Her best friends were Sam Perrone's nieces, and after her violent end, detectives found a note in her handwriting, reading, "If anything happens to me, get in touch with Sam Perrone."

Police got in touch with Perrone. "Never heard of the dame," he said.

Two years later, in 1947, her husband Louis went on trial and was cleared. The murder remained unsolved.

Private eye Sam Henderson talked so much about Perrone and Renda that Prosecutor O'Brien wished to hear more. So did his chief trial lawyer, Joseph Raschid, State Police Commissioner Donald Leonard, and Detroit Police Commissioner George Boos.

Late in 1953, Henderson's leads took him across the border into Canada. Henderson was working against time. In a few more months the six-year statute of limitations would run out and the conspirators against Reuther's life would be immune from prosecution.

North of the border, Henderson had been talking to a French-Canadian ex-con, Donald Ritchie, a loudmouth braggart, thirty-three years old, the nephew of Clarence Jacobs, another Windsor ex-con suspected of doing strongarm jobs for Perrone.

On the Friday before Christmas, 1953, Henderson told O'Brien, "Ritchie's ready to spill his guts."

O'Brien had a rendezvous with Ritchie and his mistress, Betty, twenty-seven, in a noisy Windsor saloon. From there they went to a room in the Prince Edward Hotel for a cloak-and-dagger meeting. Ritchie was either too coy or too drunk. He wasn't ready to talk yet.

Christmas came and went, and New Year's and Twelfth Night. Ritchie kept O'Brien on tenterhooks. Now he was going to talk. Now he wasn't. He showed himself a master of the element of suspense, and he insisted on all manner of safeguards. If he did talk, he wished to be kept in protective custody in a hotel. Betty, his helpmeet, was to be by his side at all times.

Finally, O'Brien got Ritchie a two-room suite on the twelfth floor of the Sheraton-Cadillac. The one concession he was not permitted was Betty. After all, the Sheraton-Cadillac couldn't wink at an unmarried man and woman consorting together openly and notoriously.

Ritchie shrugged and signed a confession. It was a quaint document. Even today it makes interesting reading.

The witness Donald Ritchie deposes and says:

I was in the car the night Walter Reuther was shot. For about four or five years I had been working for Santo (Sam) Perrone. I made about $400 or $500 a week.

In the occupation I was—well, it just wasn't what people would call work.

Clarence Jacobs approached me for this particular job. He told me I would get five grand.

I was approached about five days before it happened and asked if I wanted to go. This conversation took place in Perrone's gas station. Perrone asked me several days before the shooting if I was going on the job. I said I was.

I didn't ask a lot of questions. These people don't talk things over very much.

All I knew was that Perrone had once said: "We'll have to get that guy out of the way." Did he mean Reuther? Yeah.

The night of the shooting I was picked up in the gas station. The car was a red Mercury. I don't know who it belonged to. I sat on the back seat. Jacobs drove and Peter Lombardo was in the front seat with Jacobs.

I was there in case there was trouble. If anything happened, I was to drive the car away.

Jacobs did the shooting. He was the only one who got out of the car. I don't know how long he was gone. It's hard to remember time.

I heard the report of the gun. Then Jacobs got back in the car and said: "Well, I knocked the bastard down." We took off in a hurry.

After the job they dropped me back at the Helen Bar, about 200 feet from the gas station. I don't know what they did with the car. I heard later it was demolished and junked. I haven't any idea what happened to the gun.

I had some drinks at the bar and then went and saw Carl Renda. Why? I always went in to see Renda. He said, "I have something for you."

He got a bundle of cash and handed it to me.

I went downtown and met a girl. I stayed with her until four in the morning. Then I took a taxi to Windsor. I didn't count the money until I got to Canada. It was exactly five grand.

Everybody woke up again and began talking about the shootings. People remembered Renda was driving a maroon Ford in April 1948. He resembled the man seen running across Victor's lawn in May 1949.

O'Brien ordered Perrone, Renda, Jacobs, and Sam Lombardo arrested. Warrants went out for four John Does, the unnamed big wheels behind the attempted assassinations. Lombardo was found to be doing a stretch in Leavenworth. The cops grabbed Renda in Grosse Pointe. Jacobs was lodged in Windsor jail to await extradition.

The authorities, happy, busily sewed up the loose ends.

On the afternoon of January 8, while Detectives Wayne Glisman and William K. Krupka chatted in the Sheraton-Cadillac suite, Ritchie suddenly announced he was going to take a shower. Wearing his hat and coat, he walked into the connecting bath. The guards listened to the water running for an hour. Then they looked in just to be sure.

The water was merrily splashing in an empty bathroom. Ritchie had gone out by the other bedroom door. O'Brien gnashed his teeth. The bird had flown the coop.

Ritchie went over the border into Windsor, where he met Betty, and on to Chatham, where he bought a car for $1,400. By this time, the reader will have gathered that Ritchie was a witty crook, a sort of François Villon character, and when he bought a car, he bought a maroon sedan, like that used in the Reuther shooting. He couldn't get a Ford that color, or a Mercury, so he settled for a 1952 Dodge. After buying the car, he deposited $3,500 in the bank.

Where did Ritchie get this money? That will be seen shortly.

For seven days Ritchie and Betty eluded the police. She was picked up in Preston and soon afterward Ritchie surrendered, announcing he was repudiating every word of his confession and fighting extradition to the last writ of habeas corpus. Now that his prize pigeon was out of the cage and in a rebellious mood, O'Brien withdrew a request for the extradition of Jacobs and Ritchie.

Renda, who had been nursing his wounded vanity in Wayne County Jail, sued the UAW and several police officials for millions, claiming Ritchie had dreamed up the whole story to mulct UAW officials out of their dough. The UAW admitted that it had tried to put over a fast one on the police. It had deposited $30,000 in escrow for Ritchie in Windsor. He had taken a down payment of $5,000, was to get ten grand more when the four John Does were arrested and the rest when the lid of the case was nailed down tight.

Renda put a lot of the blame on Henderson. He said the private eye had spent hundreds of dollars on Ritchie, plying him with wine, women, and song and promising him a cut of the reward money. He quoted Betty as saying Henderson had coached Ritchie for a week before the swindler came back to Detroit with O'Brien and made his "confession."

Detectives Glisman and Krupka were given lie-detector tests and suspended for thirty days when the results showed they were not crooked but merely stupid. The Michigan Legislature extended the statute of limitations for another four years. Somewhere in the tangled evidence of this chapter lies the truth of who shot Walter Reuther. And the keepers of the peace in Wayne County worked feverishly in the hope of finding it before the new statute of limitations ran out on April 20, 1958.

Early in 1958 Renda's suit for false arrest came up for trial. One of the key witnesses was to have been Ralph Winstead, who had been investigating the Walter Reuther shooting for almost ten years.

Suddenly Winstead disappeared. A few days later his body, in fisherman's garb, was found in frozen Lake St. Clair. The coroner gave a verdict of accidental death—a death which may have sealed for all time the full story of who shot Walter Reuther.

On Top of the Heap

ᗷACK in 1945, President Philip Murray of
the CIO began to feel that he was getting old. A good
many strikers had hit the bricks since the day a wiry, sandy-
haired Irish lad born in Scotland had come up out of a
Westmoreland County, Pennsylvania, coal mine and taken
a swing at a cheating weighman.

That was in 1904, and the sandy-haired lad had been
fired for instigating a brawl on company property.

To the lad's amazement, the miners staged a strike and
elected him president of their local. A sheriff's squad broke
up the strike and put the young man on a train for Pittsburgh.

From that moment Philip Murray knew his destination.
"I never had a doubt where I was headed," he said.
Pittsburgh was the capital of the world of coal and steel,

and Murray got a job with the United Mine Workers, went on to organize the Steelworkers, and in time succeeded John L. Lewis as president of the CIO.

But, by 1945, Murray was feeling the hot breath of the Big Fellow. His sight was failing, his breath came short, and his heart did flipflops inside his skinny frame.

As far back as 1945, behind closed doors at the CIO conventions, they talked of a man to take over from the ailing Murray, and after 1947, as Reuther strengthened his hold on the UAW and wedged deeper into the CIO palace guard, they talked more frequently in terms of a man who could beat the redhead.

No love had been lost between Lewis and Reuther, and no love had been lost between Reuther and Murray, who was Lewis's righthand man in the CIO, as he had been his righthand man in the UMW. As early as the sitdown strikes of 1936 Reuther had rubbed Lewis the wrong way and produced sparks. Lewis had wanted his Steelworkers to strike first, and had always felt that Reuther had jumped the gun with his sitdown strikes at General Motors.

Again in 1945 and 1946, Murray, a "pure and simple" unionist of the Gompers stripe, had disliked Reuther's "phony economics" and Socialist attempts to gear pay rises to profits. In 1948, when Emil Mazey was acting president of the UAW, Steelworkers' Secretary-Treasurer Dave McDonald criticized a settlement with GM.

McDonald said, "I am, with all the vigor, disdain, condemnation and disgust I am able to muster, opposed to the terms of contract recently negotiated between the UAW and General Motors."

Although Murray was ailing, he was also tough and hard, and he went on and on, talking quietly in his Scotch burr, and there was still a twinkle in his eyes. Early November

1952 found him in San Francisco on his way to the CIO's annual convention in Los Angeles. On the night of the ninth he had dinner with 600 Western Steelworkers and reminisced to a late hour before retiring to his room in the Mark Hopkins Hotel.

At 6:30 A.M. a bellhop rang to awaken Murray. The man had been told to ring several times because Mrs. Murray was hard of hearing. He did. He rang eight or ten times before deciding something must be wrong. On entering he found Mrs. Murray sleeping soundly. Crumpled on the floor between the twin beds lay Philip Murray, dead at sixty-six of a heart attack.

Death came to Philip Murray on the seventeenth anniversary of the founding of the CIO. Outgoing President Truman and incoming President Eisenhower paid him tribute, and President Benjamin F. Fairless ordered one minute of silence through the great empire of U.S. Steel. The CIO voted to create a $1,000,000 foundation in his name. Some great American generals have been honored with less.

Having taken care of Philip Murray's memory, the Steelworkers started their politicking to name his successor. Their choice to assume his mantle was British-born Allan S. Haywood, who, as we have seen, was Lewis's watchdog at the Buffalo convention of the UAW in 1941. Haywood, chunky CIO executive vice president, had come out of the UMW with Murray and remained his close associate.

Reuther also girded for battle. He was the underdog, and that was the kind of a battle he liked. The quick, crisp, heady campaigning in smoke-filled hotel rooms, the low persuasive talks, the give and take of arguments were like meat and drink to him. He loved the challenge, the exchanges, the banter. He was getting good at brash, effec-

tive repartee. After election he met Eisenhower, victor over
Adlai E. Stevenson, who had been Reuther's man, and
when Eisenhower boasted he had put in many a twelve-
hour work day as a boy, Reuther quipped, "General, you
should have joined the union."

The CIO had never had a fight for its presidency. In
the seventeen years of its existence it had had only two
presidents, Lewis and Murray. Now it was going to have a
fight it would remember for many a day, with the brawling,
lusty Steelworkers leading one pack and the brawling, lusty
Auto Workers egging on the others. It was Walter Reuther
against Allan S. Haywood, Joe Curran against Mike Quill,
Dave McDonald against Emil Mazey, with no holds barred,
and God help those who were caught in the middle.

The voting went right out onto the floor at Atlantic
City, scene of earlier Reuther victories. Most of the big
international and national unions, led by the UAW with
thirty-four delegates, went for Reuther. The influential
Newspaper Guild went along with them, and one year later
Reuther would kick in with a $100,000 slush fund so that
the reporters could support the striking stereotypers against
New York City publishers—a strange manifestation of "freedom of the press."

While the big unions went for Reuther, the small ones
went for Haywood, 117 to 10. But the big ones were the
ones that mustered the delegates, and when the tally was
complete it showed Reuther the victor, 3,079,181 to 2,613,-
103.

It was a bitter fight. There had been a lot of kicking of
shins under the table, and it left scars. Some talked of unity,
but no member of the defeated coalition offered to make
the vote unanimous for Reuther. Haywood did his best to

make things look good on the surface. He led the 600 delegates in singing unity songs that brought tears to the eyes of many.

Secretary James Carey even introduced a resolution urging Reuther to drink a glass of beer and smoke a cigar as "it is noted in all history books on American labor" he did when elected president of the UAW.

The diehards were unimpressed. They wanted Haywood to refuse reelection as executive vice president and retire to a cushy job in the Steelworkers Union.

It was hard for the oldtimers to accept the new order. Lewis, Murray, and Haywood had been miners. So had William Green, president of the American Federation of Labor. Now, with the CIO's election of Reuther, first representative of the mass-production industries, and the AFL's election of George Meany, a beefy ex-plumber, a new era was opening up in American labor.

Of one thing CIO members could be certain, they never had a more dedicated leader. Murray was getting $40,000 a year when he died. Some presidents of unions, such as John L. Lewis, were getting as much as $75,000 a year. Reuther announced he would accept no salary in addition to the $11,250 the UAW was then paying him.

In his acceptance speech, a masterpiece of oratory, Reuther referred to the Carey resolution urging him to drink a stein of beer and smoke a cigar and said he was "compelled as a matter of physical necessity to say that the last resolution you adopted is beyond my capabilities."

He committed himself to seek a merger between the American Federation of Labor and the CIO, advocated a guaranteed annual wage, and outlined an ambitious program of social, economic, and industrial reform. He said:

I was sitting there with "Sandy McGregor," Allan Haywood, during the count. There were a number of votes that both he and I could understand, and when they were cast I said, "I knew that was for you," and the next one he said, "I knew that was for you," but when the Brewery Workers and Bartenders voted for me we were both somewhat puzzled. Then he got the macaroni workers—the United Macaroni Workers, let it be known, and I think that during that roll call we all had the feeling and the spirit of the CIO. . . .

Our enemies have been watching the proceedings of this convention from the cocktail bars of the Union League Clubs and the millionaires' clubs all over America. Reading the stories in the press of the division in CIO has filled their hearts with hope, filled their minds with designs to take us on if we are divided, drive us back and rob us of our hard-won social and economic gains. I say to the men who sit on the plush cushions in the Union League Clubs of America, I say this for you who are delegates, and I say it for the millions of CIO members back home, that the fat men on the plush cushions are wrong. We are not going to go out of here divided; we are going to go out of here united to carry on this struggle until we win.

In the halls of government we shall speak with one voice. We shall stand together at the collective-bargaining tables, doing the practical work on the bread-and-butter front, and when the reactionary elements are unwilling to give the workers of America, through collective bargaining in good faith, their just rewards, I say we shall exhaust every means of resolving these issues across the bargaining table through the use of logic and reason, but, failing to get economic justice through that process, we shall march together on the picket lines of America getting what is rightfully ours.

Now, there is some talk that we have division in CIO between the big unions and the small unions. Nothing could be farther from the truth. . . . We want to help build the little unions. . . .

I take no credit in a personal sense for the fact that I am a trade unionist. I was raised in a trade-union family. My father was the international representative of the Brewery Workers Union. He was president of the Central Trade and Labor Assembly in our home town when he was twenty-three years old. We got trade unionism, we got the struggle and the hopes and aspirations of working people every day.

I was raised in the kind of trade-union atmosphere that said to me when I was a boy that a trade-union movement based upon principles of pure and simple trade unionism could not adequately deal with the complex problems of the working people in the world in which we live. Our labor movement is a labor movement which integrates our efforts with the efforts of the whole people to move ahead in finding a practical and democratic solution to the complex problems that beset us. . . .

There is a revolution going on in the world. The Communists didn't start that revolution. It is a revolution of hungry men to get the wrinkles out of their empty bellies. It is a revolution of people who have been exploited by imperialism to throw off the shackles of imperialism and colonialism, and to march forward in freedom and independence. It is a struggle of the have-nots to get something for themselves. The Communists didn't start it. They are riding its back. . . .

You see, man is an economic being. He has to have food and clothing, housing and medical care and all of the other material needs, and we struggle to make that possible. But man is more than an economic being. He is a spiritual being, and just as food is needed for the economic man so the spiritual man needs food, and freedom is food of the soul. The great challenge in the world is to find a way so that man can so arrange relationship of one to the other within one society, and one nation to another in the world society, so that we can live at peace and harness the power of technology and exploit our resources and translate that into a good life for everyone . . .

They cheered him. He had won some of them over. Not all of them. No man could do that.

The Big Test

DONALD R. RICHBERG has written in his excellent study, *Labor Union Monopoly:*

> Fifty years ago the picture of a labor union as a weak, idealistic organization of downtrodden workers struggling against an oppressive concentration of property power was often accurate. Any such picture of an established union today is not merely ridiculous; it is willfully or ignorantly untruthful.
>
> Today the greatest concentrations of political and economic power in the United States of America are found—not in the overregulated, overcriticized, overinvestigated, and overtaxed business corporations—and certainly not in their hag-ridden, browbeaten, publicity-fearful managers. The greatest concentrations of political and

economic power are found in the underregulated, under-criticized, underinvestigated, tax-exempt, and specially privileged labor organizations—and in their belligerent, aggressive, and far-too-often lawless and corrupt managers.

While Americans were keeping their eyes on Big Business, Big Labor crept in and made off with the jelly tarts. Roscoe Pound, former dean of Harvard Law School, says in his study of legal immunities, "Labor leaders and labor unions now stand where the king and government and land-owner and charity and husband and father stood at common law."

The great British lawgiver Blackstone once wrote, "The King can do no wrong." Now, Pound points out, for the word "King" you must substitute "labor union," for today it is the labor union that can do no wrong.

Pound charts the disappearance through the years of the traditional immunities, and then notes that a new species of privileges has sprung up through labor legislation and court interpretation—"things which no one else can do with impunity."

Such privileges, he says, permit organized labor and its members "to commit wrongs to person and property, to interfere with the use of highways, to break contracts, to deprive individuals of the means of earning a livelihood." They also permit unions to "control the activities of the individual workers and their local organizations by national organization centrally and arbitrarily administered beyond reach of state laws, and to misuse trust funds."

Legal remedies are available to persons whose land is trespassed upon, but such right of injunction is denied employers when unions trespass upon them during a dispute. "Interference by pickets with streets and highways, which would be a nuisance if done by ordinary people, is an everyday matter," and there is no effective legal remedy for assaults on drivers, the overturning of trucks and breaking of windows and destruction of carts, or bombing of shops and houses.

The Wisconsin State Supreme Court has found that officers, members, and agents of the UAW, Walter Reuther's UAW, have kidnaped persons attempting to enter the Kohler plant in Kohler, Wisconsin, and forced them to go to strike headquarters where they were admonished against entering the plant to work or told to give an explanation of why they had absented themselves from the picket line.

Nonstrikers have been beaten—kicked in the groin—roughed up—shot at—beaten to death. One persuader on the UAW picket line, who broke a man's neck, has been a fugitive from Wisconsin justice for three years because Governor Mennen Williams will not sign his extradition papers.

Dean Pound, who reaches these conclusions in his study, *Legal Immunities of Labor Unions,* is, as financial writer Lawrence Fertig points out, "the outstanding legal scholar in the United States, honored throughout the world. His conclusions cannot be brushed off lightly."

The gift of almost unlimited power to labor unions reached its height when the U.S. Supreme Court handed down its decision in Hunt v. Crumbock, 325 U.S. 821. The union had refused to permit its members to work for a hostile employer and refused at the same time to allow his employees to join the union.

Such a plot to punish an employer, the majority of the Supreme Court said, was a proper use of the unrestricted rights of concerted action which federal law has invested in labor unions. Dissenting from this, Justice Robert H. Jackson said: "This Court now sustains the claim of a union to the right to deny participation in the economic world to an employer simply because the union dislikes him. This Court permits to employees the same arbitrary dominance over the economic sphere which they control that labor so long, so bitterly and so rightfully asserted should belong to no man."

Walter Reuther had seen the unions throw the shadow of monopoly power deeper and darker across the land, and, confident that the UAW had grown to a giant's stature, he plunged into his greatest battle.

Now, strange as it may seem, the great corporations are not the ones who offer the strongest resistance to labor unions. The officers are too fearful of the directors, and the directors too fearful of the stockholders, the stockholders too fearful of their investments.

The only obstacles in the path of the union-monopoly steamroller is the strong family company, and on April 5, 1954, when, in his second year as CIO president, Reuther struck the Kohler Company, he picked a tartar.

Anyone who looks carefully at a map of the State of Wisconsin can find, fifty miles north of Milwaukee, the small Lake Michigan port city of Sheboygan, and near it the even smaller village of Kohler. It is said of the first French explorer to the region, one Jean Nicolet, that he put on Oriental robes before going ashore because he thought he was landing in China. But, if Nicolet could land there today, more than 300 years after his initial visit, he might suspect that he was in one of the German states, for there was a heavy migration of Germans to the state after 1850 and many sections of it retain a Teutonic flavor.

The Kohler Company, second largest manufacturer of plumbing ware in the country, was founded by one of these

German families in 1873. John M. Kohler was its first president, and his son, Herbert V. Kohler, has devoted all his energy to the company since 1913. The Kohler family, specifically of Austrian stock, has been active in Wisconsin politics for eighty years, and Herbert's half-brother, Walter J. Kohler, and his half-nephew, Walter J., Jr., have held the governorship.

Back in 1913, when Walter J. was president, the company started to build the model community of Kohler which is a little village of beautifully landscaped homes, about 500 of them, and slightly fewer than 2,000 inhabitants. Most of the Kohler workers own these homes, or homes in Sheboygan. If they are unmarried, they may live in the American Club.

In the fall of 1933 an independent union, the Kohler Workers' Association, was formed in the plant. One year later the American Federation of Labor attempted to organize the employees. Obviously, the organizers could not use the common inducements, because Kohler workers were the highest paid in their whole trade and already had pensions and other fringe benefits. They had good, clean jobs and lived in a model community. In the matter of pay, for example, Kohler workers in 1954 were getting $87.45 a week as compared with an industry-wide average of $76.04 and the Kohlers were pioneers in pension and insurance benefits and other employee plans.

No, obviously the union organizers couldn't let this go on and keep their argument that all good for the American workman springs from the labor union. So they began to invent grievances. They charged that Kohler hired spies to watch the workmen. Yes, the workmen owned their own homes, but there were strings attached. The Kohlers were

German patroons, and the workmen who lived in Kohler were little better than peasants.

The AFL picketed the plant in force to prevent workers from entering the plant. At the request of the Kohlers, the state militia was called out to disperse the pickets and in the rioting that resulted two pickets were killed and forty hurt on both sides.

From 1934 to 1952 the independent union represented Kohler workers, although organized labor never gave up its intention of winning over the workers by fair means or foul. Beginning in the mid-1940s the UAW used every tactic of infiltration and argument to win over the employees. In 1951 the UAW lost an NLRB election. Employees would not voluntarily surrender good wages and conditions to force compulsory unionism on themselves or to force the company to accept union control over its management.

In 1952 the UAW tried again, and this time, by a narrow margin of less than four per cent of the votes, it won the NLRB election to represent the 4,000 employees. The contract which resulted ran until March 1, 1954, but when the UAW demanded a new contract, it served notice that it wanted a union shop. Now the reluctant employees would be forced to join the UAW, or they could go and find jobs elsewhere, no matter how many years they had worked for Kohler.

The UAW also demanded that there be no shop rules, no changing in working hours, and no subcontracting work granted without its approval. Wage progression was to be automatic, without merit increases, and promotion was to be on a strict seniority basis without regard to fitness.

The company, which had always paid better than other firms in the trade, looked upon these noneconomic demands as "union attempts to take over the functions of management." It refused to consider the union's demands, a strike was called, and what followed was a fifty-four-day reign of terror.

Striking employees, with imported hoods and goons riding herd on them, walked lock step before the main gate of the plant, to prevent other employees from going to work. Workers who tried to force their way in were roughed up and repulsed. There was an orgy of mass picketing, rioting, and widespread individual violence. The four-man police force of the village couldn't cope with the situation, and the sheriff's deputies merely ate UAW doughnuts, drank UAW coffee, and chatted with the professional organizers and strike leaders from Milwaukee and Detroit.

On the third day of the strike Emil Mazey, who called himself the "Patton of the Picket Lines," appeared to take charge of this 2,500-man picket line. With him he brought such notorious gorillas as William P. Vinson, John Gunaca, Jess Ferrazza, Guy Barbour, James Fiore, and Donald Rand.

Vinson caught one Kohler worker name Willard Van Ouwerkerk on a shopping tour in nearby Sheboygan Falls. A big, strapping 200-pounder, Vinson seized the smaller Van Ouwerkerk about the neck from behind, jammed his knee into the small of his back and jerked so hard that the older man fell unconscious to the floor. In a sadistic exhibition Vinson kicked the man and tromped on him, with the result that he lay for months, between life and death, with a crushed chest and internal injuries, including a pierced lung.

When Judge Ferdinand Schlichting sent Vinson to jail for what nearly was murder, Mazey ordered a general boycott of the chain stores in which the judge had a financial interest.

Gunaca is wanted for breaking the neck of William Bersch, a worker who had refused to join the strike. Governor Williams refuses to sign the extradition papers so that Gunaca can be returned to Wisconsin to stand trial for murder.

Pictures have been taken showing Ferrazza and Fiore mauling workers with reinforced gloves, and Rand kicking, gouging, and kneeing. This is an old story with Ferrazza. There is a historic photograph taken on April 3, 1941, showing seven men brutally beating Melvin Bartling, a timekeeper, at Gate No. 4 of Ford's River Rouge plant. Ferrazza is one of those in the photo.

In Kohler, UAW goons kidnaped nonstrikers, beat and kicked men in the groin, trampled on their chests, dynamited automobiles and buildings, fired shotgun blasts through windows, hurled acid and paint bombs into workers' homes, smashed automobile windshields, poured sand into gasoline tanks and crankcases, phoned threats to the wives and children of nonstrikers, tied weights to cornstalks so as to ruin farmers' corn cutters, and mutilated cows. These union torturers did not have to tip their hats to the terrorists of the French Revolution or the musclemen of the Al Capone underworld.

It was one long riot for almost eight weeks, even after the Wisconsin Employment Relations Board ordered the strikers to "cease and desist." The WERB had to apply for a court order, which the UAW fought all the way to the U.S. Supreme Court.

The WERB decision limited the number of pickets and dissolved the blockade at the factory entrances, and when it became assured that the Attorney General intended to act on it, the union agreed to obey the order. Once the lines were open, workers came streaming back into the plant, which soon was working at better than eighty per cent of capacity.

But, although forced to remove themselves from the plants, terrorists merely transferred their activities elsewhere. A worker returning from the job might find a mob of 200 to 500 entirely surrounding his home. For him it was like running an Indian gauntlet. He was pushed, shoved—first from one side, then from the other. The mobsters gave catcalls, Bronx cheers, sometimes even spit on him. If he got home without injury, he found his wife and children terror-stricken and often listened to obscenities yelled at him, and dirt and gravel hurled against his windows long after dark. There were 800 specific acts of vandalism of this type.

After an experience of this kind, or after being kidnaped and taken before one of the chief goons for a tongue-lashing, it was hard to keep on working. But hundreds of men and women did. As a matter of fact, the labor force grew at Kohler, and, week after week, the strike went on, but the company's production went on, too. The top officers of the UAW and the CIO were in the fracas. Walter Reuther and Emil Mazey were two men who could not afford to take a beating. The law had stepped in and told them they could not picket the entrances to the Kohler plant. But Kohler relied on the port of Sheboygan for materials. Maybe the UAW and the CIO could picket that.

On July 5, 1955, a Norwegian ship, MS *Fossum*, loaded with ceramic clay from England, which Kohler requires in its manufacturing process, entered the port of Sheboygan and attempted to unload. A Buteyn tractor, hauling a flat-bed trailer carrying a Kohler crane and manned, incidentally, by Buteyn employees, tried to enter the dock area but was prevented by a mob of 500 to 600 CIO goons. They beat one company employee. Roman Grunewald was chased a block and beaten. When the hoodlums had knocked out several of his teeth, and he lay in his blood in the street, he was let up only on his solemn promise never to work for Kohler again.

The mob halted all vehicles, twenty-five or more, including police cars. Many of them were stoned and overturned.

Instead of ordering the rioters to disperse, Mayor Rudolph J. Ploetz and Police Captain Steen Heimke told the mobsters that, if they would break up, the crane would be taken "back to Kohler where it belongs."

"I want it understood that I am not trying to prevent the Kohler Company from unloading the clay boat, but am primarily concerned with protecting the people of Sheboygan from injury or even death through a riot," Mayor Ploetz said in a statement echoing Governor Murphy's words of almost twenty years before.

After Ploetz declared, "Regardless of how long that boat remains here, it will not be unloaded," the owners ordered the MS *Fossum* to proceed to Milwaukee, where it arrived on July 7.

On the ship's arrival, Wisconsin's president of the CIO, Charles M. Schultz, threatening a general strike of 50,000 CIO members, said, "It would be a disgrace to labor in Milwaukee if the ship were unloaded here."

Although an official of the Mayor's office had observed, "This vessel was chartered by the Federal Government and we must consider our obligations to the Federal Government to service it," the Harbor Commission voted against unloading the vessel at the municipal dock. The Commission advised, instead, that the MS *Fossum* return to Sheboygan and its owners seek relief in the courts.

So it was that Reuther was able to close the ports of Sheboygan and Milwaukee to a federally chartered ship owned by Norwegians and carrying ceramic clay purchased from a British concern.

Unable to discharge its cargo, the MS *Fossum* turned about and headed down lake, back toward Montreal. Meanwhile, a second Norwegian ship, the *Divina*, unable to get assurance it would be unloaded at Sheboygan or Milwaukee, also headed back toward Montreal.

On July 16 Montreal authorities announced they expected no interference with unloading. On the eighteenth both the *Fossum* and the *Divina* docked, and next day Constable Réal Laviguérir gave pickets ten minutes to disperse; longshoremen put the clay ashore.

As it turned out, the clay still had a long, rough road to travel.

The city commission asked the Grand Trunk Railway to reroute the cars carrying the clay around the city of Muskegon, Michigan. When Walter Scowles, UAW regional representative, said, "We will do everything we can to stop the clay shipment," and spotters were posted along the right of way to watch for it, officials of the railway came back with the declaration they would move heaven and earth to protect the railway as a common carrier. The Greater Muskegon Chamber of Commerce declared, "The harbor is not a tool for labor dispute," and the union cut bait.

In Sheboygan once again, however, this time at the Union Avenue crossing on the south side of Sheboygan, pickets carrying anti-Kohler placards and marching in a tight circle blocked the tracks and frightened the locomotive fireman.

"I've got two babies," he said. "I've been reading the stories about this and I'm scared."

Next day the Wisconsin Governor, Walter J. Kohler, who had been leaning backwards because of his name, took action and ordered the UAW to lay off that freight shipment, but what the frightened fireman on the North Western switch engine had said was a fit commentary on the effect of picketing, violence, intimidation, and property destruction brought to Kohler and Sheboygan by Reuther's and Mazey's goons.

"There is no neutrality in this for us," Mazey said. What he meant can be supplied by a statement he once made under oath. "I want to state," he once testified, "that for a number of years we have been assisting sister local unions when they are in difficulty. What took place in Clinton, Michigan, has taken place in a number of other communities for the last ten years. I have been in Flint, I have been in Pontiac, I have been in every section of the state assisting our local unions to settle their problems with management, and this is the only time that people seem to have gotten excited in this particular hysterical era that we are living in today with the Taft-Hartley Act."

By the end of 1955 a bruise had been inflicted on Kohler that might never be healed. It was a bruise as disfiguring as the foul public curses and dirty words of insult chalked on some of the homes and fences. "Bastardly scab" was the least revolting of them.

Even to this day, fear rides the village like a witch on a broomstick. You must use care if you would report an act of assault or vandalism to the police chief. "Get plain paper and envelopes," he advises, ". . . use a typewriter, do not sign your name! Sign with a number, tear off a corner of your letter, curved or jagged, so that later the two pieces might be matched . . . mail to police."

As the year 1955 came to a close, it was evident that the Kohler Company, by every ordinary standard of measurement, was winning the strike. Kohler does not make its annual report public, but some indication of its earnings can be gained from income-tax returns.

In 1953, the last full year before the strike, Kohler paid $390,509 in income taxes. Even during 1954, when all production was halted for practically two months, and the village of Kohler was torn by violence and vandalism, the company made a profit and paid $124,144 in taxes.

And in the year 1955, when there was only token picketing because of the state ban, Kohler paid an income tax of $455,261.

The union could not keep pouring money down a rathole. Already the union had spent $8,000,000, and by the end of 1956 it would be $10,000,000 to break the company's stubborn resistance. Reuther had to do something, and he had to do it fast.

In the early months of 1956 the situation at Kohler deteriorated rapidly. In March, after three hours of bitter wrangling between Lyman Conger of Kohler and Emil Mazey of the UAW, with U.S. Mediator Robert Moore trying to separate them in the clinches, negotiations broke down once and for all. Three weeks later, the president of Local 833 told striking employees they had better look for other jobs.

The financial effort to break Kohler was the biggest the UAW had ever undertaken. The strike benefits alone were a great strain on the union's $22,000,000 emergency fund. Each striker received $15 a week for food for himself and his wife, and an added $3 for each child. The UAW also paid the rent or interest on the mortgage, and gave each striker $25 a week for routine living expenses.

At one time it was supporting more than 2,000 strikers. Such a dissipation of funds couldn't go on forever. In April 1956 strike benefits were reduced, and the disillusioned workers, told to find other jobs, started drifting away, some commuting to work in Milwaukee and others, estimated at about 300, moving out of Sheboygan and Kohler for good.

By every normal standard, Reuther and the UAW had lost and the towel should have been in the ring. Reuther refused to give up. He must go on fighting, and the only weapon left open to him was a national boycott. Every member of organized labor would be enlisted in the movement. All 16,000,000 AFL-CIO members, for the two were now affiliated, would take an oath not to touch a Kohler bathtub or turn a Kohler faucet.

The boycott could not be an instrument for victory. Reuther had enough sense to realize that. But it could be a weapon for punishment, a destructive bludgeon in the hands of organized labor. "It seems to me," said Donald Rand, "that it is almost sinful to have any labor dispute degenerate to the point where this one has—where we actually have to wreck the company. That's what we are doing, wrecking the company."

The union plan was simple, blunt, and terrifying. It would try to unsell Kohler products as fast as the company's sales representatives tried to sell them. Special representatives went to work seeking support for the boycott in fifteen regions across the country. Sixty-five strikers in Sheboygan started writing and distributing pamphlets and leaflets. Other unions, employers, contractors, and architects were enlisted in the boycott effort.

Bulletin boards in 77,000 affiliated unions offered nylon

T-shirts, neckties and buttons labeled "Don't Buy Kohler" and "Support Kohler Boycott." Radio commercials rapped Kohler with rhyming sarcasm.

Here and there the campaign paid off. Government bodies adopted boycott resolutions in Lincoln Park and River Rouge in Michigan; Bristol and New Britain in Connecticut; Boston, Lynn, and Worcester in Massachusetts, and Los Angeles County in California. So did the Massachusetts House of Representatives. Los Angeles county later rescinded its boycott.

Resolutions were proposed, only to fail, in New Haven and Norwalk in Connecticut; New Bedford in Massachusetts; Eau Claire, Fond du Lac, Green Bay, Jonesville, Jefferson, Salem, Sheboygan, Stevens Point, and Wawatosa in Wisconsin; Virginia in Minnesota and Pueblo in Colorado.

Waterbury and Ansonia in Connecticut, and Menasha in Wisconsin, adopted resolutions only to rescind them later.

The boycott naturally has had some effect. The Los Angeles County General Hospital in California canceled an order for $100,000 worth of Kohler fixtures. The UAW threw pickets around St. Luke's Hospital in Milwaukee, and construction workers refused to cross the picket line. Again in Los Angeles a municipal housing development was pressured out of a Kohler contract.

An exultant union spokesman yah-yahed, "Threatening to vote against certain officeholders clogged a thousand California sinks."

It was the same political threat that kept the sheriff from interfering with the original blockade of the Kohler plant in 1954.

So the Kohler war continues on a national scale, and people who may never see Wisconsin in their lives are drawn into the dispute.

"The boycott?" says Lyman Conger. "Why, it's not hurting us a bit. It's helping us. It helps us for the obvious reason that it makes people angry. Nobody wants to be told what to buy and what not to buy. That turns people against the union, and they get so they insist on Kohler products."

"We expect to be in business for a long time," says Herbert V. Kohler.

That could be. After eight months of boycott, Kohler still paid $336,856 in income taxes for the year 1956.

During 1955 Reuther's UAW tried to shoot its way into all four plants of the Perfect Circle Company in Indiana. Although the firm employed not more than 2,000, two and a half times that number massed on the picket lines. At the New Castle plant it reached its height when shots were exchanged for two hours. Eight were wounded. On October 10, Governor Craig declared martial law and 100 non-strikers were escorted out of the besieged New Castle plant. The National Labor Board ordered decertification elections at three of the plants, and the UAW was defeated in all three. Finally, the strike was settled at the fourth plant with a ten-cent-an-hour increase, and even that barely carried, 86 to 72. The union won few of its demands on other issues.

The Crow Cries, "Gaw, Gaw"

In the fall of 1954 Walter Reuther announced, "We are going to have a guaranteed annual wage." He made the statement brashly, confidently, as though a guaranteed annual wage were the most natural thing in the world. He seemed to know he was going to get a guaranteed annual wage. He had nursed the idea from infancy.

As far back as 1944 he had expressed himself through the CIO Political Action program, which said: "We can and must continue full production and full employment for men and women alike in the postwar period. A substantial increase in the income of the American worker must be the immediate objective of postwar planning and policy. The guaranteed annual wage is one means to this end. . . ."

In March 1951 he had warned in *The Annals of the American Academy of Political and Social Science:* "The guaranteed annual wage is next on our schedule in the

UAW-CIO and certainly it constitutes one of the most important tools in finding the answer to full and continuous employment in a free society. . . . Corporation executives get paid by the year; why not a worker?"

Again, in September 1953, he was telling 25,000 union members and friends at a Labor Day rally in Akron: "We've got our eye on a guaranteed-annual-wage goal that will allow the wife of a worker to plan a 52-week budget just as the wife of an executive does. We don't want to be paid for not working. What we want is to shift the burden of full employment off the backs of the workers onto the employers, where it belongs."

At the 15th Constitutional Convention of the CIO in November 1953, he said in his opening address: "One of the problems we will face shortly is the guaranteed annual wage. And we say to the captains of American industry, we don't see how you can oppose the guaranteed annual wage because that is exactly the way you pay yourselves."

Reuther was careful about the way he planned his campaign. He linked the guaranteed annual wage with two other principles. One was automation. Industry, he said, was using more and more machines, self-operating monsters equipped with electronic brains and longer than football fields. Unless something was done to guarantee wages, these machines, he said, could throw workers out of their jobs by the thousands.

There is not space to go deeply into the merits of Reuther's argument here. It appeals to the emotions, but not to reason. More and better machinery is a vital part of industrial progress, and as such has created new jobs, not destroyed them. The only destruction is in the temporary and local sense. The village blacksmith disappears with technological progress, and so do wainwrights, wheelwrights, and manufacturers of buggy whips. In their stead appears a whole, vast new industry, the automotive industry, with all the hundred and one corollary businesses, automobile accessories, road construction, gasoline refining, tire and auto-seat supplies, motels, summer and winter resorts, and roadside stands.

Only a horse-and-buggy era can guarantee security to the village blacksmith.

So much for Reuther's argument, which nonetheless sounded good to auto workers who were worried over specific jobs. They knew automation could kill them.

The other principle Reuther connected with the guaranteed annual wage was his socialistic scheme of industry councils or national planning boards, which, beginning as early as 1940, he had advanced in connection with many plans.

"It will take more than sound reasoning and proved need, however, to win this demand," he said of the guaranteed annual wage. "There are technological problems involved in the smoothing out of traditional peaks and valleys caused by seasonal production. Cooperation of management will be required to facilitate the necessary research, groundwork, and preparation for launching a wage-payment system that will give the worker a guaranteed annual wage. We intend, therefore, to call upon representatives of management to join with our union in the establishment of a Labor-Industry Wage Commission in our industry to study all possible ways and means of achieving a guaranteed annual wage that reflects equity for all workers and protects our basic contract standards."

Of course, all this was hogwash. In his demands for a guaranteed annual wage, Reuther automatically had the workers on his side because of the magic word "security."

For security, men marry women they despise. A craving for security prodded man out of his prehistoric swamp and drove him along the rough path that has led to the uplands of civilization.

In leisure moments he has dreamed of a Utopia in which he might satisfy his wants without subjecting himself to the whipsaw of risk and the flail of adversity. Plato in his *Republic* thought it might be done through the rule of philosophers; Thomas Hobbes in his *Leviathan,* through the commonwealth; and Samuel Butler in his *Erewhon,* tongue in cheek though it could be, through the elimination of all machinery.

There never was any logic behind the UAW's argument for a guaranteed annual wage. By definition a commercial enterprise is risk. A businessman manufactures a commodity in the hope he can sell it at a profit. At the same time he can guarantee nothing, for his whole commercial existence is merely the will to stay in business.

As one industrialist, Henry G. Riter, 3rd, president of the National Association of Manufacturers, said, "It is not guaranteed, it's not annual, and it's not a wage."

How, then, did Reuther, in the spring of 1955, win a form of guaranteed semiannual layoff pay, or wage, first from Ford and a week later from General Motors?

The redhead explained in very simple language how he did it: "We decided General Motors was the easiest place to get money from, because it has the most, but the most difficult to pioneer with principle. Ford is the easiest place to make progress on principle. So we decided on the strategy of implementing the principle we expected to establish at Ford with the money we get from GM."

General Motors, he said on another occasion, is "the fattest goose" in history.

Negotiations opened in April 1955, and Reuther made his pitch for GAW.

"This is something we will never, never do," Ford Vice President John Bugas said as they sat down to negotiate.

"Never say never," Reuther replied.

The Ford negotiations went on, and General Motors, which also had started negotiations, offered a stock-sharing plan.

When Ford made a similar stock offer, Reuther blew his top.

Leaning across the table, he shouted at Bugas, "How the hell do you get a Chevvy on a Ford assembly line?"

When Ford stood by its proposal, Reuther brought about a showdown.

"We're both interested in greater security for Ford workers, aren't we?"

Bugas nodded yes.

"You're convinced the workers prefer your plan, right? Bugas nodded yes again.

"All right," said Reuther, "Let's put it to a vote, your plan or ours, in a secret vote conducted by the Honest Ballot Association, or some other independent outfit."

Reuther said afterwards his proposition stopped Ford in its tracks. He knew young Ford was susceptible. Ford had turned over management of the half-billion dollar Ford Foundation and its lefthanded offspring, the Fund for the Republic, to a collection of ADA, One World, and National Association for the Advancement of Colored People sympathizers, of which Reuther was one. Ford wanted approval of the liberals and he couldn't get it by playing Scrooge to the United Auto Workers.

In the closing stages of negotiations Reuther talked tough. While Detroit newspapermen set the stage with stories that a strike at Ford was inevitable, the inside dope was that Reuther had the battle well in hand.

The redhead painted a realistic picture for Bugas. He told the Ford negotiator it was a crippling strike that had started the decline of the great Willys-Overland Company. Bugas was reminded that Chrysler was drawing up on Ford as the No. 2 automotive producer in the country until a 102-day strike put Chrysler out of the running in 1950.

Reuther was brimming over with confidence. He had bowled Ford over on the pension question in 1949, and he felt sure he could bowl over Ford on the GAW issue in 1955. During the next two weeks he slept only two or three hours a night. He lived and thrived on excitement.

In the corridor outside the conference room, where, as the strike deadline approached, unshaved, rumpled newsmen waited up all night, one veteran Detroit reporter grinned and said, "The Big Boy enjoys nothing so much as making a monkey out of the fat cats."

Noon approached—the noon when workmen were to file out of the mile-long Rouge plant. The radio played the theme song of the threatened strike, "Dance With Me, Henry." In the conference room, after twenty-six hours of hard, continuous bargaining, Reuther and Bugas stood up. They stood silent, staring at one another. Suddenly, Reuther's intent, grave face split in a grin. He held out his hand to Bugas. "You've got a deal, Johnny," he said.

If Reuther didn't have his guaranteed annual wage, he had the principle. He had won a guaranteed semiannual layoff wage.

While the newsmen were phoning their stories, the two top negotiators posed for news photographers. Bugas was drawn, harried. He looked as if he had been dragged out of the conference room through the keyhole. Reuther, despite the long, hard session which had taken them around the clock, and then some, looked like one who had just stepped out of a cold shower. He grinned again and again, his tongue pressed against the back of his front teeth, like a kid pitcher who has just won his first World Series game.

"How do you win negotiations like this, Walter?" That was one of the questions he was asked.

"You keep maneuverability," he said airily. "The art of collective bargaining is truly the art of timing and maneuverability. You have to know when to move. By maneuver I don't mean compromise. I mean the ability always to leave yourself elbow room. At the point that you're rigidly locked, everyone is in trouble. In a sense, that's the problem of a cold war—too many rigid positions. . . ."

For several minutes he dwelt on the international situation, and when he had solved the questions of global strategy, he returned nimbly to his discussion of bargaining techniques.

"Management had no maneuverability. They were so certain they wouldn't have to yield in this GAW thing in any form they hadn't done their homework. So now that Ford has given us the principle of GAW, General Motors will have to grab the Ford package in a hurry. They have no time to make any changes.

"Now, go back to Ford. Ford offered us a stock-purchase plan. We immediately saw it was the same as the one GM had offered, and we rejected it. Ford thought they had us in a box. But within thirty minutes I had already figured how we'd get out of that position."

The most ignored man in the room was John Bugas.

Reuther went on to talk of future plans.

"We'll shoot for a shorter week," he said, "but how much shorter is impossible to say now. These things can't be arbitrary. We are not a narrow pressure group seeking advantage at the expense of others in the community. A shorter work week must flow from the fact that science and technology will have given us tools to create greater wealth with less effort and time.

"Personally, I'd favor a four-day, thirty-two-hour week over six hours a day, five days a week. Then you begin to give people the real benefits of progress through a long weekend."

Someone asked, "When will labor cease asking for more?"

"You know, we go to the bargaining table and management asks, 'Don't you ever get tired of asking for more and more and more?' The answer is, as long as science and technology through the creation of abundance makes more not only economically just, but makes more and more economically necessary—the answer is yes, we are going in year after year and ask for more and more and more because we are entitled to more and more and more."

"But won't labor ever be convinced it has won its fair share?"

"That is like asking when will the human race be satisfied it has made enough progress. Labor, like other people, will continue to seek the good life. If science and technology make more possible, labor will seek to share in the increased abundance."

Somebody wanted to know, "What about the distant future?" The question appealed to Reuther and he took off soaring.

"The possibilities of human progress are as unlimited as the creative genius of the free human spirit. We are now approaching a point where man becomes less an economic being and more a cultural being.

"In the future, it's possible that the average worker will spend less time making Fords, say, and more time working on a concerto or a painting or scientific research."

At this point several newsmen stared at Reuther to make sure he was serious. He was.

"Today a guy bucking the Ford assembly line is not expressing anything of his individual personality. Relieve him of the problem of taking wrinkles out of empty stomachs and he'll be free to become creative.

"Technological advances will make that possible. In the future, an auto worker may work only ten hours at the factory. Culture will become his main preoccupation. Working for a living will be sort of a hobby.

"We'll never know how much genius went unborn because of the sheer human task of feeding families. We'll never know the Pasteurs or Edisons or Rembrandts or Marian Andersons who never had a chance."

Would the president of the CIO care to predict when the golden age of factory-workers-composers will begin?

"I don't know," he said, and he had to grin in spite of himself. "But it will come much sooner than the National Association of Manufacturers expects."

After this peripatetic discourse on the future of the American factory worker, Reuther went off for a night's sleep before tackling GM on the morrow.

In the columns of those who followed the ADA-CIO-New Deal line, Ford was hailed, approvingly, as a "traitor to his class." Nothing could be farther from the truth. If anything, Ford had protected the interests of the super-rich. The Big Two of the motor industry could roll with the blow of GAW. What they lost in extra costs would be offset by the long-term erosion of smaller rivals.

What a future generation will miss is the practical impossibility of creating new motor-producing companies. There could never be another Henry Ford. The Ford Company settlement had seen to that.

The Wild Blue Yonder

THIS, then, is an appraisal of the man.

Walter Reuther is a man of plans and planning: in his own words, the architect of the future. He has made himself the master of the Democratic Party in Michigan. His machine there is infinitely skillful, well-financed, and experienced. He tells the Governor of the State not to extradite a UAW goon to Wisconsin for beating a Kohler worker almost to death and the goon is not extradited. Now that he has become the political strategist of the merged AFL-CIO, his operations on the national level will become more and more apparent.

His enthusiastic friends and determined critics agree on the power of the man. His friends say his capacity to lead is immense, his critics complain that he carries on his back the clawing monkey of ambition. He describes himself and his lieutenants as the vanguard of tomorrow. In the words of Chester Bowles at a testimonial in the Astor Hotel, when Mrs. Roosevelt honored Reuther for his leadership, he has "spearheaded the American dream." In the language of the New York *Herald Tribune* he is "a dangerous and disingenuous opportunist" and "reckless politician" dynamoed by "aggressive demagoguery."

Writing in the London *Telegraph,* July 22, 1957, Daniel Bell of Columbia declared, "The coming man is Walter Reuther," who is "disliked for his puritan morality and feared for his ambitions." The writer says, and correctly, "Industry, too, fears Reuther. . . . But the paradox is that increasing attacks on labor by industry can only force more aggressive response, and the only one strong enough to maintain an aggressive posture is Reuther."

The poet laureate of Americans for Democratic Action, Arthur Schlesinger, Jr., asserts in his book *The Vital Center,* "Walter Reuther, the extraordinarily able and intelligent leader of the United Auto Workers, may well become in another decade the most powerful man in American politics."

J. B. Matthews interprets this as meaning that Reuther seeks to become President, which, in the words of the song, ain't necessarily so, because Reuther could look upon the office of President as another rung to power. When Schicklegruber the housepainter has become Hitler the Reichschancellor, he can still aspire to becoming Hitler der Fuehrer.

Reuther is a man applauded for puritanical morals. This Sir Galahad of the labor leaders, it is said, does not dip snuff, imbibe intoxicating liquors, wager on the horses, shoot craps, stick his hand into the union till, or use obscene language. People say his objectives are good. So were

Benito Mussolini's when he tried to make the railroads run on time. It was not until later that people began to notice the bodies left along the right of way.

Walter Reuther, in Walter Reuther's estimation, is, without exaggeration, a latter-day Moses whose self-appointed task it is to lead the oppressed out of capitalistic bondage into the Promised Land of socialistic planning, full employment, and guaranteed income for all. A crusade such as his pays off only when the people are willing to sacrifice personal initiative and responsibility for security. Indeed, the failure of our representative republic, if it should fail, would result from the readiness of most of us to live from day to day as dependent serfs under a feudal system in which political and economic overloads guarantee our security for the privilege of predetermining our destiny. Too many of us are ready to sacrifice the rewards of initiative, incentive, and hard work for the various forms of individual and collective welfare and security dreamed up by ambitious men.

Among these ambitious men, Walter Reuther stands high. He is a superb pitchman whose spiel postulates and embraces the equality of man, the redistribution of wealth, the brotherhood of man, all the timeworn shibboleths which have marked the Communistic thinker since the days of Karl Marx.

Reuther seeks to be all things to all people. Basically, of course, he is a Socialist. In the Detroit *Times* of October 5, 1937, he said, "As an automobile worker, as a union official, as a member of the Socialist Party, I pledge myself to the service of all the people." He is a doctor of Laws at Wayne University, St. Mary's College, and Boston College, Doctor of Humanities at West Virginia University and Wilberforce University, and Gaston Lecturer at Georgetown University, pretty good for a lad who flunked algebra.

In October, 1949, he addressed the third annual convention of the United World Federalists in Cleveland. He worked with the Americans for Democratic Action, the National Association for the Advancement of Colored People, and many groups of such New Deal economists as Leon Keyserling. In October, 1954, he handed a UAW check for $200,000 to Methodist Bishop William C. Martin, head of the National Council of the Churches of Christ in America, "to help finance the Council's educational program in the area of church and economic life."

In 1958, if he could have had his way, he would have forced the four-day week upon the auto industry, beginning with General Motors, which, more than two years ago, he called "the fattest goose" in history. First the Russian sputnik, then a moderate recession, intervened to make a demand for more leisure time appear ridiculous. So Reuther, ever a quick-change artist, switched to a plan for "basic economic gains" and a share of the profits.

His plan, which caught the auto companies off guard, called for them to split profits over ten per cent of net capital three ways. Half would go to stockholders and executives, a fourth to workers, and a fourth to customers as a rebate. On the 1956 figures at General Motors such a plan would mean about $530 to the average worker, equivalent to a pay boost of 26 cents an hour, well above the ten-cent-an-hour straight pay boost the GM worker is likely to get.

At the same time the average rebate to an auto customer would be $48, while dividends would be cut $290,000,000, or more than half.

Of course, the Reuther demand appeared a little ridiculous in the light of the fact that, three years before, both General Motors and Ford offered the United Auto Workers a stocksharing plan, for which they were roundly chastised by Reuther. Many financial writers were quick to point out the unfairness of the plan, which gives workers the chance of participating in the spoils without the risk of winning them or suffering loss in the case of reversals. Most observers saw little chance of the plan's succeeding, and it was the general belief that Reuther had thrown it into the hopper as a bargaining point or to confuse the issue. He also did a great deal of talking about excessive car prices, as he had done a dozen years before when he even demanded that the companies open their books to him. The president of American Motors, George Romney, openly charged that Reuther was trying to give the nation a phony price picture.

Strike threats hung in the air after the UAW executive council boosted dues from $3 to $8 a month—the extra $5 to go toward building up the strike fund from $24,000,000 to $50,000,000. The delegates were told $34,000,000 might be enough to take on Ford or Chrysler, "but we can't set up any kind of strike fund without considering General Motors, too."

Reuther would be a tough man to beat in a strike. His strike generalship shows him to be as great a master of the strategic minority as Lenin. He took over Kelsey-Hayes with a handful. Beginning with only small cadres of union men, he organized one plant after another and came from behind to win one union election after another.

Reuther is a man in whom Marxian doctrine is so deeply ingrained that it colors all his thinking. Once an applauder of the Russian experiment, he stood just outside the door of communism, but he resisted taking the final, fatal step that would have put him under party discipline. In time he learned the magic of the anti-Communist pitch and made

it his peculiar touchstone. So well did it serve him in de-
feating George Addes and going on to win the UAW presidency in 1946 and 1947 that in 1949 he decided to carry
his evangelistic torch against the Reds into the CIO.

Chief target of the Reuther campaign was Lee Pressman, who by this time had admitted the bar sinister on his
ideological escutcheon to House investigators. On Reuther's
insistence, Pressman was given the heave-ho as the CIO's
chief counsel. A calculated campaign had been carried on
against two unions which the redhead said were shot
through with communism. No one, of course, doubted the
charges for one minute against the United Electrical Workers Union and their little brothers, the Farm Equipment
Workers. But Quill's shouted charges of "pinks, punks,
and parasites" and Murray's hints at clandestine meetings
of Communist Party bosses William Z. Foster and Eugene
Dennis with UE Bosses James Emspak and West Coast boss
Harry Bridges seemed unconvincing evidence. Reuther and
others in the CIO could be tarred with the same Red
brush. One speaker at the convention pointed this out with
the statement that most of those speaking in favor of the
expulsion "are ex-Communists, ex-Fascists, and ex-Social-
ists."

He can talk till Doomsday about fighting them, but the
Communists retain a great deal of affection for Walter Reuther. The Party in 1957 passed a resolution praising Dubinsky, A. Philip Randolph, and Reuther for "performing
the function of Social Democracy."

In the June, 1956, issue of *Political Affairs,* which carries the authorized Party line, Erik Bert wrote, in comment on the Reuther plan to contribute two per cent of
the country's gross product each year to a World Fund for
the purpose of giving economic and technical aid to less

developed countries, "Reuther's two major points, taken together, provide for participation by the United States and
the Soviet Union in a common effort to bring to the pov-
erty-ridden peoples of the world the wherewithal for up-
grading of their economies."

Observers, especially Congressional investigators, should
not be surprised when they find Communists and Socialists
deeply entrenched in labor unions. Not only does the labor
union movement, by its very nature, appeal to proponents of
socialism, but from the early days of the movement Communists have played very important roles. Unity has always
been a CIO instrument of political power, and thirty years
ago unity meant a great amalgamation of labor, farmers, and
other dissident and dissatisfied voters. Of these, the Communists were the most vocal, and John L. Lewis, who needed
eloquent trained organizers, welcomed them with open
arms, thinking he could always shed them when they had
outlived their usefulness.

The Communist *Daily Worker* did most of the early
drumbeating for unity. "Pull Together—Don't Pull Apart"
was a typical *Daily Worker* headline in 1938. As recently
as 1953, four years after Murray, Reuther, and Company
had booted them out on their subversive behinds, blithe
spirits in the Communist Party still cheered for unity, offered suggestions, and hailed every move in the right direction, the right being to the extreme left.

Since December, 1955, labor leaders have talked of
unity in terms of the merger of the AFL and the CIO. After
almost three years it becomes more and more obvious that
the unity will be troubled and temporary, because AFL
leaders are unwilling to pay the CIO's high price for labor
peace.

One of Reuther's archenemies is Dave Beck, owner of

that famous house that union jack built. While it is true that Beck misappropriated some thousands in union funds for his own personal interest, Reuther has supervised the spending of close to a quarter of a billion dollars of union funds in the ten years of his UAW presidency, much of this in the pursuit of political and ideological objectives.

UAW disbursements for the year 1956 alone totaled $28,500,000. Only a voucher-by-voucher accounting would reveal how much of this went to politicians, but those who have read *The CIO and the Democratic Party* know that the CIO contributed more than $200,000, or 60 per cent of the funds which elected Governor Williams of Michigan.

James R. Hoffa, Beck's successor as Teamsters boss— over union, Congressional, and judicial opposition—is another Reuther enemy. Hoffa is a man who has made crime a legitimate union business. He went to bat for the notorious Johnny Dio, convicted extortionist and notorious racketeer of New York City's garment district, and blamed as the man who plotted the acid blinding of newspaper columnist Victor Riesel. At least a dozen Hoffa subordinates have gone to jail or paid fines for extortion, bribery, and violence against teamsters.

Hoffa has recently beaten one rap after another, one of them for trying to bribe a way for a stooge into the McClellan Rackets Committee. But that has long been the Hoffa pattern. In 1949 his probation report showed seventeen arrests for assault. He once beat a taxi driver named Edward Chevlin unconscious with auto chains because Chevlin fought racketeering within the Teamsters Union. It would take pages just to recite other charges against him.

Reuther and Hoffa hate one another, as strong men of a type hate one another. Their enmity goes back to the days of the sitdown strikes, when Reuther was leading the civil war against law and order and Hoffa, as he likes to put it, was "on the side of the law." What he means is that he just didn't happen to be violating the law at the time and the UAW men were standing in the way of the truckers who were trying to do business as usual in Detroit, Flint, and Dearborn.

They have always been on opposite sides of the fence, and each loves nothing better than to raid the other fellow's territory. Neither speaks to the other, if he can avoid it, and once, sitting side by side on a plane flight, they maintained a rigid silence from Detroit to Washington.

The notion has been seriously advanced by *Newsweek* magazine that Reuther is behind the charges of the Mc-Clellan Committee against Beck and Hoffa and that the committee's attitude toward Reuther has been one of conciliation. Why? Because the committee counsel, Robert Kennedy, fears that Reuther, if called to account for his sins, might kill off Robert's brother, Senator John Kennedy, as a possible candidate for the Democratic nomination in 1960. They remember how, at the 1956 Democratic Convention, Reuther killed off Governor W. Averell Harriman by switching Michigan's delegation to Adlai Stevenson, over Williams' mild protest.

The committee has been forced, mainly because of the insistence of the minority, and the minority's special counsel John McGovern, into making a cursory investigation of Reuther's political activity and violence in connection with the Kohler strike. But the public mustn't expect too much of Congressional investigations, even those put on with the most lavish window dressing.

Hoffa has conspired with Harry Bridges, West Coast longshore boss, to form a giant council of American transport workers—air, land, and sea. Hoffa's plan would combine all the nation's transport unions in aviation, trucking, shipping, and railroading into one great council.

"You can't have a one-city strike any more," Hoffa explains, "or a strike in just one kind of transportation."

Bridges, Communist sympathizer who, because of his domination over the insular longshoremen and plantation workers, is the first absolute ruler of the Hawaiian Islands since King Kamehameha, echoes Hoffa: "There is one thing I know. If the Teamsters and the two dock unions got together, they'd represent more economic power than the combined AFL-CIO. They are so concentrated. An economic squeeze and pressure can be exerted that puts any employer in a very tough spot. And, furthermore, puts the U.S. government in a tough spot. If the AFL-CIO meets us head on, we'll knock the stuffing out of them."

Another labor leader who will fight Reuther is Dave McDonald of the Steelworkers. McDonald was the power behind Haywood when Reuther whipped him for CIO president in 1952. McDonald hates Reuther as only a leader who came out of the Mine Workers with Lewis, Murray, and others can hate an upstart from the mass-production industries.

McDonald is the scholar of the labor leaders. Oddly enough, he worked first with Wheeling Steel Corporation, where Reuther served his apprenticeship. McDonald studied accounting at Duquesne University, but switched to the Carnegie Institute of Technology, where he took courses in physics and mathematics. Before graduation he had changed to Tech's drama school, and he took his degree in public speaking, composition, and production.

The Steelworkers' president is probably the only labor boss to study the drama. Maybe that accounts for his dislike of Reuther. It helps him to recognize a bad actor.

When George Meany became president of the AFL-CIO in 1955, he announced, "Our major objective is to elect strong, liberal minorities to Congress." Soon afterward he declared that if the National Association of Manufacturers tries to prevent workers from "expressing their views politically," they would be "compelled to start a political party."

We have seen that this threat to form a third political party is not new. At the very first UAW convention in 1936, which Reuther attended as a delegate, a resolution was passed in favor of a farmer-labor party. Lewis, who wanted the whole CIO to support Roosevelt, managed to have this sidetracked. This was pure expediency, however, because the CIO had put up $500,000 for the Roosevelt campaign, as we saw, an investment that was to pay off in the form of the Wagner Act for labor. The general belief in the need for a new party has always pervaded the CIO, and George Meany's statements only show how Reuther dominates his political thinking.

Through the war years Walter and his brother supported Roosevelt, although Victor wrote in *Common Sense* in December, 1945, "The time is now ripe for labor to divorce itself from the two old parties and resolve to build the base for an independent, indigenous, new national political party."

After FDR's death Reuther denounced Republicans and Democrats alike for "playing fast and loose with the welfare of the American people." Truman, he described as "hopelessly inadequate." In the August, 1948, *Automobile Worker,* he pledged "my full support and my full energy for a new political alignment." When the CIO supported Truman against Dewey and Wallace, however, the UAW adopted the same position.

Reuther had feared the election of Dewey, and when Truman was successful, Reuther junked the idea of an educational convention that was to have preceded the inauguration. Although he still toyed now and then with the idea of a third party, he began to devote more and more of his energy to an infiltration and corruption of the Democratic Party. After all, why should the political Louis Wolfson build himself a new mail-order business if he can take over Montgomery Ward?

On April 10, 1957, Harry Southwell, president of Local 174, stood on the platform in Atlantic City, scene of that brawling convention of more than a decade before which had first elected Reuther UAW president. It was a different scene now; somebody had nominated Carl Stellato president of Ford Local 600 and symbol of Reuther opposition. It was a bare gesture, and Stellato quickly withdrew. Reuther was elected by acclamation. He had stamped out all dissension.

Only a few days before, speaking in Milwaukee, Cola G. Parker, chairman of the board of NAM, had warned that the country faced an "autocratic labor dictatorship," with Reuther of the UAW in the driver's seat. Senator Barry Goldwater has charged that Reuther is "exploiting the labor movement to create a machine for personal political power." In the Arizona Republican's opinion Reuther has "done more damage and violence to freedom than all the peculiar financial transactions of Beck."

"There's more than one way to misuse union funds," says *Human Events*. "Dave Beck's way is to appropriate union funds for his personal ideological interests. Beck's misappropriations have apparently run into thousands of dollars; Reuther's have run into millions."

One former high government official once told me an

anecdote. The President loaned him an Air Force plane to go to Detroit for a speech. He made his talk, a good one, and a redhead came up afterward to congratulate him.

The high official accepted the redhead's extended hand. He was feeling pretty good about everything, and when the redhead asked for a lift back to Washington, the high official could not say no. Walter Reuther was still hitchhiking, but on a grander scale.

The plane was to leave at one o'clock in the morning, and the high official arrived a few minutes before the scheduled time, walked alone across the field to the plane, and climbed aboard.

At a quarter to two, forty-five minutes late, a big car roared up to the plane. Reuther, bareheaded, got out, flanked by two husky gorillas with obvious bulges under their coats.

"I can't go anywhere without them," Reuther hastily explained.

The high official had not bargained for it, but he had not one but three hitchhikers.

He told me that he sat in the plane on the way back, watching the redhead thumb through the papers in his briefcase. On both sides of him, like the two thieves, the broken-nosed, thick-eared bravos dozed. The strongarm men had taken off their coats now, and the most obvious feature of their attire was the shoulder holster.

The high government official sat there, looked at the redhead bowed over his papers, glanced one way, then the other, at the two thieves, and thought, This is the architect of the future. It reminds me too much of Al Capone. God help America.

Privately, on more than one occasion, George Meany has said this will never happen, "because Walter Reuther is a Socialist." That remains to be seen. Harry Bridges spoke the truth when he said Reuther is a very ambitious man. Too bad he has violated Joseph Conrad's rule, "All ambitions are lawful except those which climb upward on the miseries or credulities of mankind."

I understand what that government official meant. Nothing has happened to our country, at least not outwardly. No one has attacked it since Pearl Harbor. But old constitutional landmarks have vanished. The house of our government has suffered an inner decay. Fading are the beauty, dignity and strength of the structure we once knew. The flag doesn't seem to fly as high as it once did. In our newspapers and magazines we are the dupes of propaganda and pressures, and our boasted freedom is a mockery, for we are in the grip of political, social, racial, and religious forces we do not have the courage to face. We are worse than an ignorant nation. We are a grossly misinformed one.

One hundred years ago, Karl Marx set down the ten ways to achieve communism, the Ten Commandments according to his Gospel. Check them off in the Communist Manifesto from Number One—Abolition of property in land—and Number Two—A heavy progressive or graduated income tax—right through Number Ten—Free education for all in public schools. Karl Marx would be a proud man today if he could see his box score and the zealousness of public officials, taxpayer groups, neighborhood associations, and parent-teacher associations to insure that his errors go down as hits.

Our government has become more and more a welfare state which ministers to our needs and tells us what to do. We look more and more to Big Government to shelter us and to show us the way. We more readily accept manna from the Potomac, forgetful that government can give us

nothing it did not take from us in the first place, forgetful
that too much reliance on government makes social puppets
of us all. "Whose bread I eat, his song I sing" comes to us
as a warning from the England of long ago, when Anglo-
Saxons fought for the individuality and the freedom they
had felt were their heritage since the days of the Witenage-
mot.

We are about one third socialized today. Roughly one
third of our income is channeled through government in
one shape or form. If the trend continues at the rate it has
followed since 1929, we will be 99 per cent socialized in
another fifty years. Only one in a hundred will work for
himself. The others will work for the Great White Father
under the eye of Big Brother.

Day by day that Big Brother takes on a form more
nearly resembling Walter Reuther's. He has his counter-
parts working energetically abroad—Frank Cousins of the
Transport and General Workers Union in England and
Otto Brenner of the metal workers in West Germany. All
three are young, militant, persuasive, popular. They have
an actor's sense of his audience, an ability to think on their
feet, and what the London *Times* calls a "feline capacity
for destructive argument." Together, they form an all-
power triumvirate, the Triple Alliance Supreme. They could
smash the economy of the free world, suddenly, by concerted,
massive strikes; they could smother it and are smothering it
slowly with wage-rise-fed inflation.

Can they be stopped? Yes, they can be stopped, if the
industrial brains and wealth of the world stand firm, as they
have not stood firm in the last generation. If his huscarls
had stood firm at Hastings, as he had ordered them, Harold
could have beaten back William the Bastard. They didn't.
And the Bastard went down in history as the Conqueror.

Appendices

Questionnaire to be mailed January 16, 1941; to be returned January 21, 1941. It was returned on the 21st of January signed by Walter P. Reuther, order no. 774.

First joint large toe on right foot amputated. Eight years of elementary school and 4 years high school and 3 years at Wayne University, economics, sociology—labor problems.

Administrative duties at the present time—CIO; have done this for 3½ years: Salary: $57.70 weekly. Employers: International Union United Automobile Workers of America, CIO, at 281 West Grand Boulevard, Detroit, Mich., whose business is a labor organization. Other business or work in which I am now engaged is member of the National Committee on Training within Industry Division of the National Defense Advisory Council.

Served apprenticeship as tool and die maker, all type of tool and die construction—bench and machine—1924 to 1936.

Married March 13, 1936, and lives with his wife. Wife, May Wolf Reuther, age 30, receives $1,000 a year. Also claims Anna Mae C. Reuther, age 17, sister. Date when support began: September 1, 1940. $10 weekly NYA, "and it costs me to maintain my home for the last 12 months, $1,000; rents house at $60 per month."

Reuther was born at Wheeling, W. Va., September 1, 1907.

REGISTRANT'S STATEMENT REGARDING CLASSIFICATION

"My wife intends to discontinue work within the next month or two at which time she will become entirely dependent.

"Walter Philip Reuther."

Minutes of action by local board; This local board classifies the registrant in Class I, subdivision A, by vote of three to nothing—not dated.

Before returning to the official record, the following summary in the Congressional Record may help to interpret the document:

When men were being drafted for World War II, and Walter P. Reuther was called by his local draft board, deferment for Reuther was asked for occupational reason by R. J. Thomas, then UAW-CIO president.

Reuther in his questionnaire did not ask for a deferment. He listed as dependents his wife, May, who was then a UAW-CIO employee, and his sister, Anna Mae, 17.

Thomas, requesting deferment status for Reuther, gave three reasons: That he was director of the union's General Motors Department: that he was a member of the National Subcommittee on Training and Industry of the National Defense Advisory Commission and that he was engaged in speeding up airplane production through the utilization of surplus automobile plant capacity.

Reuther had received two invitations from Uncle Sam. One was from the draft board, as indicated. The other came from the OPM.

Later, in March of 1941, the draft board rejected the union's request that he be deferred because of his defense activities. However, the Office of Production Management, Monday, March 24, 1941, stated that Reuther had been recommended for an appointment for "certain consulting services or other services." It added that, while the job was without compensation, expenses would be paid while he was on Government duty.

The board held that Reuther had no dependents.

On April 30, 1941, the board gave Reuther a class I-A rating, the tentative induction date being May 21, when 42 men from the Detroit area were to be sent to the Army.

A few days later Thomas, president of the union, and Philip Murray, president of the CIO, announced that an appeal would be taken from the draft board decision. Murray stated that Reuther "has direct supervision for the union on labor regulations covering 78 plants and 173,000 workers. A great many of these employees are engaged in defense production."

Shortly thereafter the draft appeal board put Reuther in class III-A. He was given deferment because his wife, May, was dependent upon him—the board stating that, inasmuch as she was employed as Reuther's secretary, had he been drafted, she would have been out of a job and unable to support herself.

Now to fill in the rest of the strange story from the amazing draft board record:

April 29, 1941: Classified in I-A after examination by medical advisory board.

Walter P. Reuther appealed to the board of appeal on April 30, 1941. On May 27, 1941, the appeal board No. 3, by a vote of five to 0, classified the registrant in class III-A.

SUPPLEMENTARY INFORMATION
REQUESTED BY BOARD OF
APPEALS

May 9, 1941: Date of mailing was May 9, 1941—received by the local board May 19, 1941. Page 4, note: "My sister Anna Mae Reuther is no longer receiving any support from me. She has secured employment for her room and board since I filed my questionnaire on January 21, 1941.

SERIES VII, DEPENDENCY

The income I earned during the last 12 months was $3,000. The following is a list of property owned in the last 12 months: Walter P. Reuther and May Wolf Reuther home at 20101 Appoline purchased, paid $4,050, due $3,700; bank deposits Walter Reuther and May Wolf Reuther, $1,265.

No. 12: "My wife and I will move into our new home the first week in June at which time my wife will discontinue work and become entirely dependent."

May 7, 1941: Letter from board of appeal No. 3 to ex local board No. 31. This is just a letter requesting that the answers to questions on dependency be supplied. See questions 6, 9, 10 and 12 under series VII.

May 1, 1941: Letter from the local board No. 31 to appeal board No. 3: "Walter Philip Reuther has not requested a hearing but has signed an appeal to the board of appeal but simply is adding data signed by R. J. Thomas, president of the CIO, and newspaper clippings which he has filed with the board.

"After he filed his questionnaire on January 22, 1941, he filled out portions of the questionnaire but left most of the spaces blank, therefore, it was impossible for the board to determine his classification. He was invited in for a hearing on the matter of his questionnaire on Monday, February 3, 1941. He appeared at this hearing and when questioned stated that he did not think it was necessary to fill in the questions which he did not fill in, which were all those covered by pages 4 and 5, as he had filed an affidavit for deferred classification signed by R. J. Thomas, president of the CIO, which he figures was all that was necessary. When questioned he was told that from information given in questionnaire the board could not do otherwise than put him in class I as there was nothing we could find in the rules that would permit us to defer him. He then gave information that was not originally on his questionnaire, and from which we determined he belonged in class I.

"This board passed upon Mr. Reuther's classification solely upon his questionnaire supplemented by the affidavit of R. J. Thomas filed with this board January 28, 1941. You will find a request for deferment from Philip Murray, dated April 23, 1941, coinciding with the original request of Mr. R. J. Thomas, president of the CIO. You will also find a letter signed by Col. I. D. Brent, state adviser on occupational deferment. This letter was in response to telephone conversations between Mr. DeLand, Mr. Harrigan, and Colonel Brent. You will also find copy of letter, date February 7, 1941, mailed to Mr. Reuther regarding his dependency. We might state further on page 7 of his questionnaire registrant's statement regarding classification at the time of his hearing, you will note that he wrote in on the questionnaire at the same time that he filled in pages 4 and 5. At that time he notified the board that his wife was his private secretary and in the job he was holding it was utterly impossible to replace her with any other woman to do the work."

May 23, 1941: Letter from the local board to appeal board No. 3.

"We herewith submit the complete record of Walter Philip Reuther, order No. 744, consisting of request for appeal; CIO Bulletin, 8 pages of newspaper clippings; R. J. Thomas' letter, April 30, 1941; questionnaire; form 42, R. J. Thomas; medical reports; form 42, Philip Murray; Philip Murray letter, April 17, 1941, copy of DeLand letter, February 7, 1941; I. D. Brent letter, February 13, 1941; supplemental questionnaire; affidavit of board members; newspaper clipping.

"Please sign original and return to local board No. 31.
"Janet D. DeLand."

May 21, 1941: Letter from Mr. Walter P. Reuther to local draft board No. 31: "Mr. Philip Murray, president of the Congress of Industrial Organizations, and Mr. R. J. Thomas, president of the International Union, United Automobile Workers of America, CIO, have asked me to appeal my classification to the local appeal board. The request of Messrs. Murray and Thomas for my deferment is for occupational reasons, as stated in affidavits already in the files of the local board No. 31. I shall be glad to appear before the local draft board No. 31 on Friday, May 23 at 11 A.M."

(Note: This date, May 21, Reuther was to have been inducted, along with 41 others from the Detroit area. This had to be explained to the press.)

May 23, 1941: Notice to the press from the local board No. 31:

"Mr. Walter P. Reuther, order No. 744, appeared before the board today to comply with the request to get additional information as requested by the appeal board No. 3. The board has received this information and is forwarding it to the appeal board and can take no action until we hear from the appeal board."

Signed:

"Edward H. Harrigan,
"Chairman."

(Note in Congressional Record: "It seems funny that this further information should be referred to the local board prior to the appeal board, and what reasons had Harrigan for giving this statement to the newspapers as it is?")

February 13, 1941: Letter from Col. I. D. Brent to the local board No. 31:

Colonel Brent admits that he knows Mr. R. J. Thomas, president of the UAW-CIO, has submitted an affidavit and, under regulations, he (Reuther) meets their requirements as a necessary man, and in the light of this situation and in the national interest, as well as the community interest he believes it advisable that the board (local) give serious consideration to placing this registrant (Reuther) in class II-A for a period not to exceed 6 months, which is the maximum period permitted under the regulations.

                              Signed by I. D. Brent, Colonel.

February 13, 1942: Claim for deferred classification by person other than registrant. This claim was filed on DSS Form 42, signed by Philip M. Murray, and sworn to on the 7th day of April 1941. It was received by the local board April 23, 1941.

(Notice the dates)

April 17, 1941: This was a letter dated April 17, 1941, to the chairman of the draft board No. 31, signed by Philip Murray relative to the collective bargaining relationship in the plants of the General Motors Corp. at this time. This was received by the local board April 23, 1941.

(Notice the dates)

Letter of February 7, 1941, to Reuther from the local board asking more information pertaining to his wife.

January 24, 1941: Letter from the local board to the registrant directing him to appear before the local board at 10 A.M., Monday, February 3, 1941, for a hearing in the matter of his questionnaire.

May 16, 1941: Memorandum to files signed by Janet D. DeLand, chief clerk:

"I received a telephone call at 3:40 P.M. from Washington, D.C., from Mr. Reuther, explaining that he would not be back in Detroit until this weekend, and asking if we would grant him permission to file his supplementary questionnaire on Monday, May 19th. I agreed that I would take the matter up with Mr. Harrigan, Mr. Harrigan agreed to give Mr. Reuther an extension of time until Monday."

Telegram to the local board pertaining to his delay in Washington.

May 9, 1941: Letter from the local board to Mr. Walter P. Reuther: "This board has received a communication from the Appeal Board to which your appeal has been sent, requesting us to have you give further information that you failed to give in filling out your questionnaire. We are enclosing a supplementary questionnaire marked under series VIO, 'see questions No. 6, No. 9, No. 10, and No. 12' which the appeal board insists on you filling out completely. At the time you signed the appeal you were requested to state on what grounds you appealed. You declined other than verbally, which you stated was occupational, and, at that time, you submitted certain documents to accompany your appeal. The appeal board now insists on you sending in a written statement stating this information on what grounds you are basing your appeal. We would like to have this information within the next 5 days."

April 30, 1941: Received by the local board a note from Walter P. Reuther: "Please add the enclosed material to my file and refer them to appeal board."

"Walter P. Reuther."

It was a 16-page pamphlet—500 Planes a Day, a Program for the Utilization of the Automobile Industry for Mass Production of Defense Planes, by Walter P. Reuther.

Sic!

These papers were received by the local board No. 31 on April 30, 1941. The local board also received from

Mr. R. H. (cq) Thomas a very lengthy letter on the same date. Also a lot of newspaper clippings and the public reaction to same. These editorials and clippings were no doubt collected by Reuther and given to Mr. Thomas.

February 14, 1941: A letter from the chairman of the board to Col. Samuel D. Pepper:

"I enclose you herewith copy of a letter I wrote Walter P. Reuther regarding his classification. The letter was dated February 7, and up to this date Mr. Reuther has paid no attention to it that I know of except to show it to Colonel Brent. I will admit that if this board wanted to be absolutely cold-blooded, we could classify every registrant upon his questionnaire as he returns it to us, and perhaps we should do it that way, but it has seemed to us that it is more human to ask registrants who fail to completely fill out their questionnaire to do so, or ask them in to talk about their dependents, or, even in what I consider a close case, like this one, to ask for some additional information.

"It was my original idea that if Reuther's wife was about to quit work as he states in his questionnaire and as he told Mr. Harrigan, our board member, that we could then classify him as a 3-A man solely upon the question of dependency but he doesn't seem to want to cooperate."

January 21, 1941: Form 42 was filed by Mr. R. J. Thomas and received by the local board on the same date —January 21, 1941.

Highlights:

1. Mr. Reuther is director of the General Motors department of the United Automobile Workers of America, CIO. As such, he has charge of labor relations covering 69 plants and 160,000 workers. Almost all of these plants

are important in the national defense program. It is Mr. Reuther's function to keep labor relations smooth so as to permit continuous operation of these plants. He is engaged in almost daily conferences with GM executives on these problems in Detroit and elsewhere. It would be impossible to replace him with a person as responsible as he is and as familiar with labor relations machinery in GM.

2. He is a member of the subcommittee on training in industry of the National Defense Advisory Commission and as such is doing important and responsible work in developing sufficient trained personnel for defense industries.

3. He is engaged in important discussions with officers of the War Department, the Defense Commission and other Federal officials looking toward the more speedy construction of defense aircraft.

Later in 1941 Representative Clare Hoffman of Michigan, who read most of the above into the Congressional Record, wrote General Lewis B. Hershey, Deputy Director of Selective Service System, for an explanation of Reuther's draft deferment. This was General Hershey's reply.

NATIONAL HEADQUARTERS
SELECTIVE SERVICE SYSTEM
21st Street and C Street NW
Washington, D.C., August 5, 1941.
(In replying address The Director of Selective Service and refer to No. 1-8-5-75)
Hon. Clare E. Hoffman
House of Representatives.
Dear Mr. Hoffman: In accordance with your request, we have made a complete investigation of the classification

of Walter Philip Reuther, order No. 744, Wayne County
Local Board No. 31, Lansing, Mich.

It appears that this registrant at no time made a claim
for deferment on the grounds of dependency, although
his record indicated that dependency was involved. The
registrant did claim deferment as a necessary man because
of his occupation as a representative of the United Automobile Workers, an affiliate of the Congress of Industrial
Organizations.

Upon appeal of the case of this registrant, board of
appeal No. 3 at Detroit, Mich., deferred the registrant in
Class III-A on the grounds of dependency.

While it is not specifically stated in the file, it appears
that the registrant does not desire to be deferred on account of dependency but rather desires to be deferred as
a necessary man.

When a case is appealed to a board of appeal, it is in-
cumbent upon that board of appeal to consider all questions and to place the registrant in the lowest classification
justified by the evidence and information contained in
his record. Occupational deferments in Class II-A or II-B
are not as low in classification as the dependency deferment in class III-A. For this reason, the board of appeal
acted in direct conformity with the Selective Service Regulations when it placed this registrant in class III-A, as
the lowest deferment status justified by the record.

Accordingly, as the record now indicates, the registrant
is deferred and is free to carry on his occupation and
maintain those who are dependent upon him. In our view
this deferment should be entirely satisfactory to the registrant, and we believe that there is no good reason why
he should pursue any further his objection to such a

classification. In the event that subsequently his classification may be changed, by reason of a change in circumstances, from class III-A, then full consideration would be given to any other grounds upon which a claimed deferment would be found to exist.

We trust that the information contained in this correspondence is found satisfactory to your inquiry.

APPENDIX B:
Letter from Leslie Avery to Victor Riesel

August 19, 1957

Mr. Victor Riesel
610 West End Avenue
New York, N.Y.
Dear Victor:

I was interested in reading your column of Aug. 14, in which you cite the fact that German Social Democrats, using the lever of codetermination, are prying their way into West Germany's economy.

You conclude, "Obviously it would not be long before the Socialists and their partners in the German unions, the DGB, would control the revived industry which has brought almost lush prosperity to this battered land.

"And I believe that as Germany goes, so goes the rest of free Europe."

Don't you think, Victor, that America may be going in the same direction?

Aren't you afraid that some American labor leaders, notably Walter Reuther, the son and grandson of German Social Democrats, would like to get a Marxist armlock on the American economy?

Of course we're both thinking of the same thing, those industry councils.

It was way back in November of 1940 that Reuther, then vice president of the United Auto Workers, went to Washington, accompanied by Philip Murray, and put down on President Roosevelt's desk his program for aircraft production and his first plan for industry councils.

I have only to look at the front page of *The New York Times* for yesterday, Aug. 18, to see that Walter Reuther still seeks to tell industry how to run its business.

Over this seventeen-year span there have been I don't know how many so-called Reuther plans, but they've all had one thing in common—an over-all *commune concilium* which would have full control over materials, allocation of manpower, prices, tooling, facilities, new patents, the migration of farm hands, distribution of goods under "social priorities," manufacturing quotas and types of goods to be produced.

In that now famous speech of his in 1944, "Challenge for Peace," Walter Reuther said in part:

"I think that we must insist that at this time the national government, both the Administration and Congress, announce, as a matter of national policy, that in the postwar period we will permit free, private enterprise that degree of freedom necessary to make its maximum contribution in terms of employment; but if free, private enterprise fails to meet the requirements of our nation, in the terms of standards of full employment, then the government will not hesitate to take those steps necessary to insure and maintain those levels of full employment for our people.

"I think the government should create an overall

agency to regulate and begin to work out plans . . . to plan and to coordinate economic factors in our national economy . . . we have not forgotten that free enterprise did not meet the requirements of war, and it will not meet the requirements of peace."

What does Walter Reuther mean by an industry council?

In his plan for aircraft production we read on page 9:

"We propose that the President of the United States appoint an aviation production board of nine members, three representing the government, three representing management, and three representing labor. We propose that this board be given full authority to organize and supervise the mass production of airplanes in the automobile and automotive parts industry."

That was 1940. In the years since then, Reuther has risen to take Murray's place as president of the CIO, and in 1952, we find Labor Leader John Brophy getting up at the CIO convention and extolling the plan for industry councils, in these words:

"Much time has gone by since the original Plan was presented to President Roosevelt in the winter of 1940 and '41 . . .

"As World War II passed beyond its critical phases and thought had to be given to postwar plans, President Murray presented to the 1944 CIO Convention his Reemployment Programs. In adopting this program, CIO reiterated its position in favor of the Industry Council Plan, fitting it now into a peacetime context as part of our permanent policy. At nearly every CIO Convention since then, we have adopted a resolution reaffirming our stand. . . .

". . . this industrial planning program of the CIO, which we often refer to as the Industry Council Plan, or simply as the Murray Plan, is a program of comprehensive national economic planning.

"It states that the people of America through their government and their economic organizations—labor unions, farm organizations, consumer organizations—must have a voice in shaping the key decisions in the basic and monopolistic industries which affect their lives.

"It proposes to accomplish this by national planning and the establishment of representative boards called Industry Councils, one in each basic industry, and one overall national board, composed of representatives of labor, management, farmers, consumers, and government.

". . . the critical industrial decisions which must be dealt with by democratic industrial planning would have to include production levels, investment levels, employment levels, and the rate and nature of mechanization and technological change. On these matters depend the volume of employment and hence industrial stability.

"They would have to include also the establishment of stable wage floors, strict ceilings on hours of labor, firm price ceilings established through the administrative mechanisms of the corporations themselves, subject to democratic public control, and the closely connected questions of the nature and quality of goods produced.

"They would include the labor-management relations (meaning propaganda and advertising) and the foreign relations of our big corporations.

"They would include the policies of these corporations in respect to natural resources, and in respect to the size and location of industrial plants, questions which are deeply involved in all regional planning for the benefit of the people.

"Along with these controls there would be others related to public policy in providing electric power, other fuels, and also public credit. The whole program, of course, would call for the adoption of extensive and carefully designed federal legislation.

"I pointed out then and at other times that national economic planning is not new in America. The corporations have been doing their own planning at our expense for a long time. We need to put these decisions on a democratic basis by legislation providing for participation by government and the economic organizations. . . .

"We are confronted I think with an end of an epoch: the third great struggle in modern American history to take the American government and American economy into the hands of the people and away from predatory special economic interests, specifically, and particularly the big corporations.

"One of those efforts was the Granger, Greenback, Populist Movement of 1873 to 1896 which ended with the rather complete political defeat of the farmers. The second was the Progressive Movement of Theodore Roosevelt, merging into the New Freedom and internationalism of Woodrow Wilson; this movement was destroyed in World War I. The third effort has been the New Deal—Fair Deal—CIO crusade of the 1930's and 1940's, with its Resource Conservation and the Industry Council Plan."

The CIO repeatedly passed resolutions urging the creation of Murray's and Reuther's industry councils. Like Reuther's recent proposal that if the auto industry will cut prices of cars, he will shape the UAW's 1958 contract demands within the framework of the companies' financial position, the industry council is ostensibly designed to "promote industrial peace."

You know, and I know, it would place industry in a Marxian strait-jacket and forever kill the meaning of American free enterprise.

Very truly yours,

(signed)

Leslie Avery
Ass't. Vice President,
Public Relations,
Nat'l. Association of
Manufacturers

Index

273

Due